THE TSARS AND THE EAST

THE TSARS AND THE EAST

Gifts from Turkey and Iran in the Moscow Kremlin

Dr. Alexey Konstantinovich Levykin

FRONTISPIECE: *Detail of shield (cat. 5)*

Sponsors

The Tsars and the East: Gifts from Turkey and Iran in The Moscow Kremlin
is organized by The Moscow Kremlin Museums and the Arthur M. Sackler Gallery of the Smithsonian Institution.

The exhibition is presented under the High Patronage of
His Excellency Dmitry A. Medvedev, President of the Russian Federation.

Honorary Committee Chairs

His Excellency Sergey I. Kislyak, Ambassador of the Russian Federation
His Excellency Nabi Şensoy, Ambassador of the Republic of Turkey

The exhibition has received generous support from Lukoil.

Additional support is provided by the
U.S.-Russia Business Council and the Russian-American
Chamber of Commerce in the USA.

The exhibition is supported by an indemnity from
the Federal Council on the Arts and the Humanities.

First published in the United Kingdom in 2009 by
Thames & Hudson Ltd, 181A High Holborn,
London WC1V 7QX

www.thamesandhudson.com

British Library Cataloguing-in-Publication Data
A catalogue record for this book is available from the British Library

ISBN: 978-0-500-51497-9

Printed and bound in Singapore

CONTENTS

PREFACE

Elena Yurievna Gagarina

IN THE CENTER OF the Russian capital, on Borovitsky Hill above the Moscow River, stands the medieval fortress of the Moscow Kremlin. Behind its crenellated red brick walls and star-topped towers rise the snow-white bell tower of Ivan the Great, the gleaming golden domes of the Kremlin cathedrals, magnificent palaces, and stately government buildings.

The Moscow Kremlin is one of Russia's holy of holies, a unique monument of world culture where the nation's relics are protected and displayed. Centuries of Russian history are preserved in the Kremlin, which has been witness to many of the state's most significant events, from the heroism of the fortress's defenders to the victorious return of the Russian army. The Kremlin has survived internecine struggles, popular uprisings, and devastating fires. It has seen colorful royal ceremonies, grand receptions of foreign ambassadors, accessions to the throne of Muscovy's grand dukes and Russia's tsars, and impressive coronations of Russian emperors. From ancient times to the present day solemn services have taken place in the Kremlin cathedrals. Beginning in the twelfth century the Kremlin was a princely residence, and later it became the permanent residence of the Muscovite grand dukes and Russian tsars; from 1918 it served as the seat of the Soviet government. Today the Kremlin is the residence of the president of Russia, Dmitry A. Medvedev.

The Kremlin's vast collections are unequaled in their antiquity, their historical importance, and their artistic value. Chronicles and other written sources from the fourteenth and early fifteenth century provide the earliest evidence that a princely treasury was once incorporated into the Kremlin amid the architectural ensemble that today houses the museums' priceless collections.

Once part of the Tsar's Treasury, the Armory Chamber now occupies a special place in the museum complex. Contemporaries wrote with undisguised astonishment and delight of the Tsar's Treasury storerooms located in the Kremlin. Here the precious arms and armor of the tsar and his family were kept. Also transferred here were gifts from foreign rulers as well as diplomatic and trade imports from countries to the west and east. Armorers, jewelers, embroidresses, and artists applied their skills in the workshops attached to the Russian court. They produced the tsar's armor and ceremonial trappings, his

attire, and all objects necessary for the life of the court, in addition to icons and decorations for the Kremlin cathedrals and palaces. Activities in the Kremlin workshops reached their finest flowering in the seventeenth century. In the eighteenth century, with the transfer of the capital to St. Petersburg, the Kremlin workshops ceased operation and were merged into a single institution called the Workshop and Armory Chamber. The old Tsar's Treasury was gradually transformed into a museum, created by decree of Emperor Alexander I in 1806.

This exhibition, *The Tsars and the East: Gifts from Turkey and Iran in The Moscow Kremlin*, is the first in the museums' history to be devoted specifically to the Kremlin's Eastern collection. Its nucleus comprises diplomatic gifts and trade imports from Safavid Iran and the Ottoman Empire presented in the sixteenth and seventeenth centuries. Such refined works of art from the court workshops of Iran and Turkey exemplify the high levels of design and workmanship associated with those countries. Representing the rich legacy of the Kremlin masters are objects and textiles with Eastern forms, embellishments, and decorative details. Preserved over many centuries in the museums of the Moscow Kremlin, these precious wares represent a unique and valuable record of Russia's relations with her Eastern neighbors. This exceptional collection has no parallel in the museums of the world. It encompasses textiles, weaponry, horse trappings, and jeweled objects created of precious materials — in other words, items that were essential to Russian court life and were used in staging the most important official ceremonies of the state and the religious services in the Kremlin cathedrals.

The extraordinary art of Safavid Iran and the Ottoman Empire continues to be little known to the world, and this marks the first time these beautiful pieces have been presented so comprehensively in an exhibition outside Russia. Not only have some of the works never before been taken out of Russia, but also a few of them have never left the confines of the Moscow Kremlin. While their defining characteristic is the exceptionally high quality of their workmanship, the story of how each one was created and entered the Kremlin collections, as confirmed by centuries-old archival documents, further increases their historical importance.

We hope *The Tsars and the East* generates lively interest among public viewers and scholars alike, and it also fosters friendly cultural connections among our peoples.

View of the Moscow Kremlin.

FOREWORD

Julian Raby

The objects in this exhibition are the glittering remnants of the exchanges that took place in the sixteenth and seventeenth centuries between the tsars of Russia and their imperial counterparts in Istanbul — the Ottoman sultans — and Isfahan — the Safavid shahs. These exchanges were driven by the twin, and often simultaneous, imperatives of diplomacy and trade. While both of these motives are readily appreciated today, the sight of ceremonial presentations is far less familiar in a country where Congress has placed limits on the value of gifts that can be retained by the president, ever since it obliged President Martin van Buren in 1840 to sell or present to the nation some of the gifts he received from the sultan of Muscat

(today Oman), including two Arabian stallions, four cashmere shawls, a Persian rug, and a long string of pearls. Yet the exchange of lavish gifts had been the norm in most cultures for much of recorded history. Even if the Ottoman grand vizier explained, in restrained tones, to a European diplomat in 1563 that a gift was more an issue of honor than of value, the reality was that the status of a donor and the sincerity of his purpose were most often measured by the splendor of his gift. *The Tsars and the East* provides the opportunity to be dazzled by opulence and entranced by craftsmanship, but it also allows insight into the interplay of the power of panoply and the panoply of power.

A FLOURISHING TRADE EXISTED BETWEEN the central Islamic lands and the lands of the Rus as early as the late eighth century CE, lasting well into the tenth century. Evidence takes the form of the abundant hoards of Islamic silver coinage that have been found in Russia, as well as from the accounts of Arab geographers, such as Ibn Hawqal, who describe a trade from the north principally in furs but also slaves, and from the south in worked goods and silver coins. Some of the

coinage remained in European Russia, but much passed through the area on its way to the Baltic and northern Europe.

Some six to seven hundred years later, in the sixteenth and seventeenth centuries, the geopolitical picture had changed dramatically. Three great powers dominated the regions between western Europe and the Asian steppes: the Russians, the Ottomans, and the Safavids. Their capitals — Moscow, Istanbul, and Isfahan — stood thousands of miles apart, but these powers interlocked, especially in the Crimea and the Caucasus. Military and political demands prompted frequent diplomatic exchanges, increasingly so in the seventeenth century, but trade remained an ever-present factor. Indeed, many of the embassies to and from Russia and Iran or Turkey were little more than trade missions that took advantage of the "diplomatic bag" to avoid customs dues and restrictions on imports. The trade was primarily in furs from Russia and silks from Turkey and Iran. The Russian court itself and the Orthodox church were major consumers of imported woven silks, since no silk-weaving industry existed in Russia at that time. At the Ottoman court, it was considered a mark of the highest esteem if the sultan presented a robe lined with sable or ermine from Russia.

The silk trade was so important to the economies of Iran and Turkey that any attempts by the Ottomans to embargo or punitively tax Iranian exports that were being sent via Anatolia or Ottoman-held Syria strained peaceful relations. It was little wonder, then, that efforts were made to find export routes to western Europe that circumvented the Ottomans entirely. In the 1520s an Italian attempted to open a route to the Baltic via Astrakhan and the Volga, followed some thirty years later by an agent of the London-based Muscovy Company. In 1584 Ivan IV founded the port that would later be known as Arkhangelsk (Archangel) on Russia's northern seaboard, with an aim of creating a direct north-south route to Iran. Russia was both a destination and a transit route for Iranian and Ottoman silks, acting, as it had so many centuries earlier, as a conduit for trade with the Baltic and northern Europe. From the first decades of the seventeenth century, however, the growing presence of the English and Dutch in the Indian Ocean and the Persian Gulf ensured an alternative southern outlet for Iranian silks and carpets.

Playing a prominent, though by no means exclusive, role in this trade were Greek merchants from Istanbul, who were often designated Ottoman court merchants, and Armenians operating on behalf of the Safavid court. As Christians, the Greeks and Armenians enjoyed an advantage in dealing with the patriarchal establishment of the Russian church in Moscow, and many of the finest objects in this exhibition were gifts to the patriarch or were made specifically for the Orthodox clergy in Russia.

It is no small wonder, then, that with these international exchanges Eastern modes of dress and display exerted a considerable impact on court aesthetics in Moscow. I am most grateful to our colleagues at The Moscow Kremlin Museums that they agreed to incorporate a closing section of this exhibition that touches on Middle Eastern elements in the expression of a Russian style. These range from Iranian and Ottoman items being absorbed into the tsar's Grand Attire to the adoption of "Turkish" designs

and metal inlay techniques. These influences extended to the ecclesiastical realm, and it is fitting that one of the final items is a "panagia" with an image of Christ carved in a Byzantine style set in an Ottoman jeweled mount. The Russians looked to Istanbul, the famed city on the Bosporus, as the seat of the Orthodox patriarch of Constantinople as well as the capital of the Ottoman sultan.

For understandable reasons many of the most important historical items in The Moscow Kremlin Museums cannot be lent to exhibitions outside Russia. These include the imperial regalia, a Safavid gold and jeweled throne given by Shah Abbas I to Tsar Boris Godunov in 1604 (see fig. 9), the "diamond throne" of Alexei Mikhailovich given by the New Julfa Armenian Trade Company in 1660, and a bejeweled and enameled crown and scepter made in Istanbul almost certainly in 1658.

Even without these exceptional items, this is a dazzling presentation with an unprecedented array of loans. A few of the objects were featured in two of the greatest exhibitions of Islamic art ever assembled — the one held in Munich in 1910, and the "Exhibition of Persian Art" in London in 1931 — but most of these works have never been presented together in Europe or the United States. We are enormously proud to have been offered this opportunity, and our experience with working with our colleagues from The Moscow Kremlin Museums has been a pleasure from start to finish, from my initial discussions with Deputy Director of Exhibitions Zelfira Ismailovna Tregulova, my several visits to Moscow to confer with Dr. Elena Yurievna Gagarina, Director General of the Kremlin's museums, and to meet with the Deputy Minister of Culture, Mr. Andrei Busygin, to our sessions with Kremlin curators, especially Olga Ivanovna Mironova, Olga Borisovna Melnikova, and Inna Isidorovna Vishnevskaya, in which they revealed the treasures of their storerooms and discussed with an affecting devotion and intimate knowledge the works of art kept there. Working with the team in the Kremlin's International Department has also been a delight. In short, our colleagues in Moscow have been generous in the extreme, from securing support for the exhibition from Lukoil to taking sole responsibility for the main essay and entries in this catalogue.

Lukoil has been a most generous sponsor, at a time when support for the arts has been sorely affected by the economic crisis. I would like to thank Mr. Vagit Alekperov, president, and Mr. Igor Beketov of the Lukoil Charity Foundation.

We are most grateful for the enthusiastic support we received from His Excellency Sergei I. Kislyak, Ambassador of the Russian Federation to the United States. His Excellency Nabi Şensoy, Ambassador of Turkey, and Mrs. Şensoy have similarly lent their support, building on a relationship between the Turkish embassy and the Sackler Gallery that started with the very successful exhibition *Style & Status* in 2006.

Special thanks go to Cultural Attaché Natalia Batova and to Irina Khortonen at the Russian embassy for their many good ideas and repeated efforts to make this exhibition a success. Ed Verona of the U.S.-Russia Business Council and Sergio Millian

of the Russian-American Chamber of Commerce in the US, and the staff at their respective organizations, made sure every corporation with an interest in Russia learned about the exhibition. Guy Archer of the American Chamber of Commerce in Russia promoted the exhibition to the members of the Chamber.

On a personal note, I would like to thank Nicolas Iljine, and one of my oldest friends, Richard Wallis, and his wife, Lyuba Shaks, for their generosity when we were in Moscow and for introducing us to so many inspiring people.

This exhibition covers material in which I have long had an interest, and if I have one regret it is that I personally have not been able to devote the time to it that I might have liked. This is where I owe a special word of thanks to our curator of Islamic art, Massumeh Farhad, who somehow has managed to incorporate the needs of this exhibition into a year full of other demands. I would like to thank other staff members of the Arthur M. Sackler Gallery and the Freer Gallery of Art, particularly those in the design and publications department, for all their help and for a job well done.

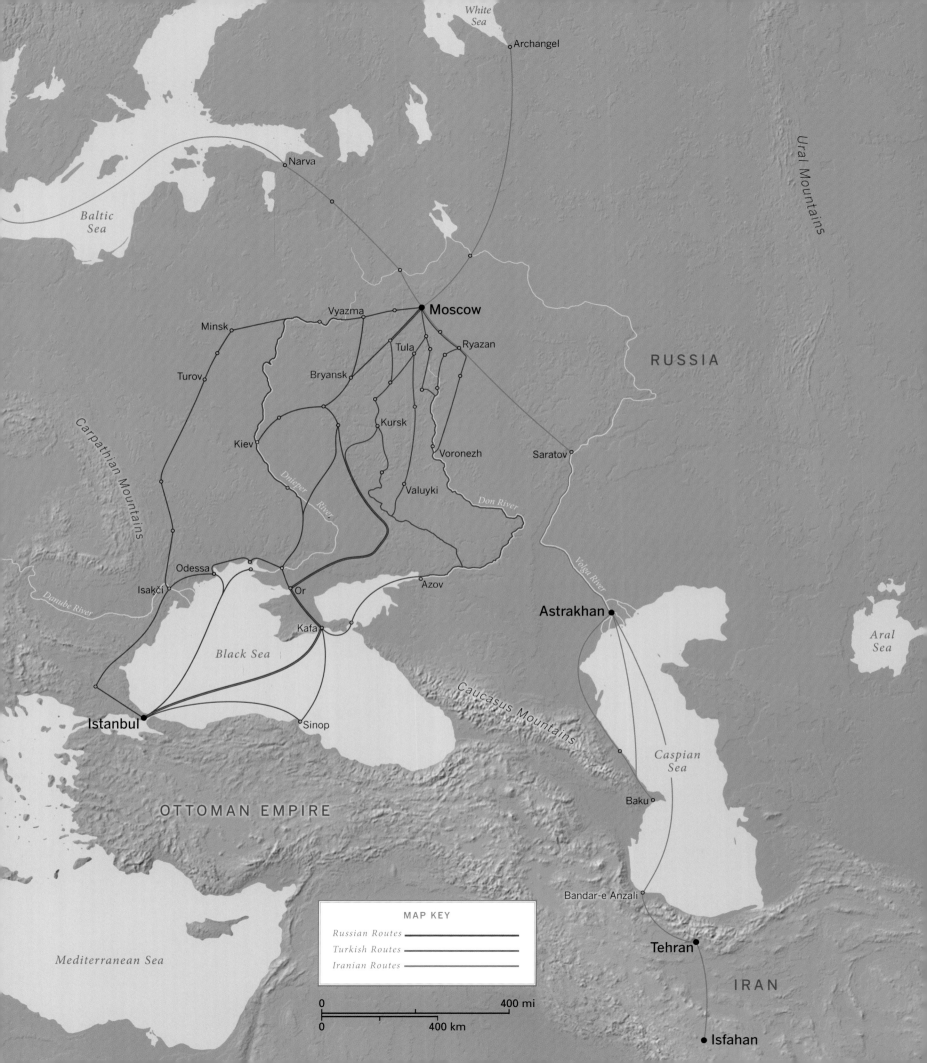

White
Sea

Archangel

Ural Mountains

Baltic
Sea

Narva

RUSSIA

Moscow

Vyazma

Minsk

Tula

Ryazan

Turov

Bryansk

Kursk

Kiev

Voronezh

Saratov

Dnieper River

Valuyki

Don River

Carpathian Mountains

Volga River

Odessa

Or

Azov

Isakči

Danube River

Astrakhan

Kafa

Black Sea

Aral
Sea

Sinop

*Caspian
Sea*

Caucasus Mountains

Baku

Istanbul

OTTOMAN EMPIRE

Bandar-e Anzali

Mediterranean Sea

MAP KEY

Russian Routes ——————

Turkish Routes ——————

Iranian Routes ——————

Tehran

IRAN

Isfahan

0   400 mi

0   400 km

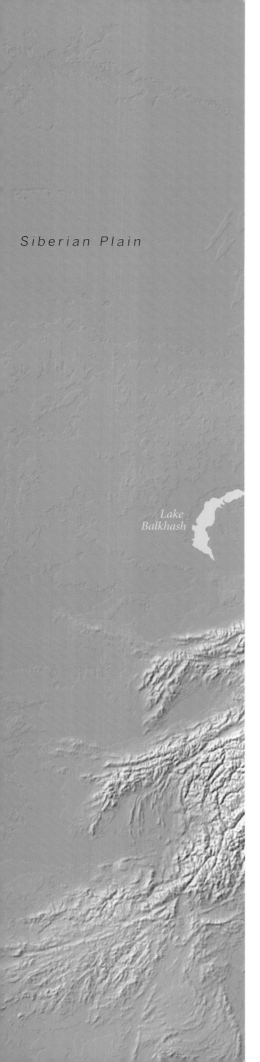

Siberian Plain

Lake Balkhash

TRADE ROUTES

In the sixteenth and seventeenth centuries Russia's expanding trade relations with the Safavids in Iran and the Ottomans in Turkey grew in commercial and political significance. Merchants in western Europe attempted to establish profitable transit routes through the Volga basin to Iran, thereby bypassing the traditional routes through Asia Minor. Russians responded by strengthening their own trade agreements with Iran and acting as intermediaries between Europe and Iran. Formal trade relations between Russia and Turkey were established in 1495 and reconfirmed in 1613, when Tsar Mikhail Fedorovich assumed the throne. Russian merchants were allowed to trade freely throughout the Ottoman Empire, and Turkish traders frequently brought their goods to Moscow.

Eastern Treasures
of the Russian Tsars

Inna Isidorovna Vishnevskaya

The Eastern treasures of the Russian tsars are a unique collection of objects, historically shaped by the Russian state's cultural interactions with neighboring countries. It includes ceremonial arms and armor, magnificent horse accouterments, objects made of gold and precious stones, and luxurious textiles. The principal part of the collection comprises items presented to the Russian tsars in the sixteenth and seventeenth centuries by Iranian shahs and Ottoman sultans as part of diplomatic and trade contacts. Another group of objects was given to the tsar by his intimates at court, while other works entered the Kremlin Treasury from the escheated property of distinguished boyars (Russian nobility) and

leading government figures. In certain instances the court simply purchased goods in Iran and Turkey. In 1623 Ivan Kondarev and Tikhon Bormosov, the Russian ambassadors to Turkey, were instructed to buy in Istanbul items especially for "the tsar's use."[1] Later, in 1663, Kirill Demidov, an undersecretary to the Privy Treasury, acquired in Iran an enormous quantity of fabrics for the court at a cost of 73,586 rubles 18 *altyn* 2 *dengi*, a huge sum for that time.[2]

Eastern items brought from abroad were for the most part housed in the Tsar's Treasury, which functioned as a state treasure house, and were recorded in its inventories. Moreover, their visual specifics were meticulously noted. At the end of the description were listed the price and, if known, the date of acquisition and the name of its presenter. All objects released from the Tsar's Treasury and their subsequent use were also carefully noted in its income and expenditure books and its inventories. On the basis of all these archival resources, a large portion of the Iranian and Turkish objects from the Kremlin's collections can be precisely dated, which makes them important sources for correlating works with objects from other museum collections around the world.

The array of impressive objects in the Eastern collection of the Russian tsars shares several distinguishing features. Entirely absent, for instance, are examples of ceramics, illuminated manuscripts, or objects associated with Islam. This fact is extremely interesting from historical and cultural points of view in that it clearly illustrates the kinds of imported Eastern goods that were in great demand in Russia from the fifteenth through the seventeenth century. Some of them entered Russian court life; others had a more mediated purpose. Arms and armor and horse trappings were used unchanged in the most important state ceremonies. Russian tailors and embroidresses transformed a large percentage of the yards of Eastern textiles that entered the Moscow court into a variety of items utilized in Russian daily life. Secular dress, church vestments, and many items for ceremonial court interiors were created from imported Eastern fabrics. They were also used to make horse blankets, to upholster saddles, and to line shields and armguards. As a distinctive kind of semifinished product, numerous Turkish gold plaques set with diamonds, rubies, and emeralds were imported into Russia, where they were utilized to decorate a variety of Russian goods. From Iran came the unique watered steel saber blades forged by the celebrated armorer Rajab-Ali Isfahani (cat. 6, 7) and were regarded by the Muscovite court as particularly fine examples of blades.

Some of the earliest works from the Moscow Kremlin's Eastern collection are connected with the art of the Golden Horde. While this term conjures up the luxurious golden tent that signified the headquarters of the Great Khan, it is actually of Russian origin. It appeared in the Russian chronicles to describe the territory of Ulus Juchi, part of the vast state that emerged as a result of the Mongol invasion in the twelfth to fifteenth centuries, which placed many Russian principalities under vassalage. The capital of the Golden Horde was Sarai Batu (Old Sarai), founded by Batu Khan in 1254 on the lower Volga River. Later the capital was moved to the city of Sarai Berke (New Sarai) on the middle Volga. The Golden Horde's economic flowering was based on trade between the countries of the East and the Far East and the territories of Central Asia. Artifacts found in archaeological excavations of Golden Horde cities testify to the significant growth of a local culture and to the establishment of centers that produced both functional and artistic wares. Local artists assimilated the traditions of Mongolian culture that had been preserved primarily in court customs as well as many aspects of the cultures of those peoples who lived in the widespread territories controlled by the Golden Horde, that is, the Volga Bulgars, the Polovtsians, Slavs, Persians, and Greeks. The ethnic make-up of Golden Horde craftsmen was international. Russian masters comprised a vast colony in Sarai Berke, for example, and the Russian craftsman Koz'ma served as a court jeweler to Güyük Khan, grandson of the empire's founder Genghis Khan. Indeed, Koz'ma created the throne and personal seal of the Great Khan.[3] After attaining its greatest flowering under Uzbeg Khan, the Golden Horde underwent a period of decline that was precipitated by the Battle of Kulikovo in 1380 and the campaign of Timur in 1395. According to several contemporary scholars, however, after Timur destroyed Sarai Berke many Golden Horde craftsmen found refuge at the court of the Muscovite grand dukes.[4] In the fifteenth century the Golden Horde fragmented into the Nogay Horde and the Kazan, Crimea, Astrakhan, and Siberian khanates, all of which subsequently became part of the Russian state.

Golden Horde craftsmen most likely created the seal ring (fig. 2) that is traditionally linked with the names of Alexei

Metropolitan of Moscow and the khan's wife Taidula, whom the religious leader cured of blindness in 1357. Made of greenish copper, this ring has a pale stone set in a round mount and carved with the poorly preserved image of a four-legged animal. Depictions of similar animals are found on many fourteenth-century Eastern coins.[5] In the fourteenth and fifteenth centuries such rings served as the personal seals of the khans of the Golden Horde.

The name of Metropolitan Alexei is closely linked to the history of Moscow's rise to prominence and the consolidation of power. He served as the de facto regent to Grand Duke Dmitry Ivanovich during the young man's minority. Through his strong authority he helped the prince to subdue feudal unrest and preserve state unity. The metropolitan played a role in almost every aspect of Moscow politics in the 1360s.

Metropolitan Alexei actually visited the Golden Horde and its capital, the city of Sarai Berke, in 1357. By the sixteenth century a widely disseminated tale recounted how Metropolitan Alexei was summoned to Taidula, the ailing wife of the khan. After her miraculous cure, the khan of the Golden Horde bestowed numerous favors, including this ring, on the esteemed representative of the Russian church.

The most senior and favorite wife of Uzbeg Khan and mother of Janibeg Khan, Taidula took an active part in foreign policy in the 1350s by corresponding with foreign sovereigns and dispensing her own charters. The fact that she distributed such documents testifies to the significant role she played in the Golden Horde, thanks to her exceptional personality and the constant support she received from a coalition of clan princes. Leaders of Christian states, well aware of her role as a "defender of Christians" at the court of the Golden Horde, constantly sought her aid.

As a multinational state, the Golden Horde remained religiously tolerant for a long period. In 1261, the year in which Berke Khan converted to Islam, an Orthodox diocese was established in Sarai Berke, with its embassy church (*podvor'e* or metochion) located in Moscow. Another unique object from the era of the Golden Horde is the gold cover (*oklad*) on the icon of the Mother of God Galaktotrophousa (cat. 1), a sixteenth-century copy of the ancient Barlovskaya Mother of God, which has not survived. The gold *oklad* shown here initially covered this earlier icon, which was one of the most venerated objects in the Annunciation Cathedral of the Moscow Kremlin. The central part of the *oklad* is embossed with a pattern in which the word "Allah," written in Naskh script, figures repeatedly. Scholars who have studied this work believe the embossed gold strips (*basma*) may have been made with the participation of Golden Horde craftsmen in the fourteenth century in Moscow. Also attributable to Golden Horde jewelers of that time is a set of *basma* silver plaques sewn on the yoke of a phelonion, donated, so legend has it, by Tsar Ivan IV (the Terrible) to the Protection of the Virgin (Pokrovsky) Convent in the town of Suzdal. Some of the smooth plaques are shaped like scrolling clouds and have clear Chinese overtones, while those stamped with the image of a *senmurv* (dragon) can be equated with motifs from Turkic mythology. Interestingly, the dragon became the heraldic emblem of the Kazan khanate, which was formed after the Golden Horde was subsumed within the Russian state by Ivan the Terrible in 1552.

At its apogee the state associated with the reign of the Timurid dynasty encompassed the lands of Iran, Central Asia, Armenia, and Iraq as far as the Euphrates, and traditionally it has been linked with the history of Iran. An embroidered wide collar (*oplechè*) from a ceremonial garment (cat. 3) may have been created during that era. Angels or peris holding various vessels used for feasting are embroidered with fine gold lamé threads, multicolored silks, and "bird of paradise" feathers. These motifs closely parallel Iranian miniatures of the Herat school from the fifteenth century, which suggests that artists from the court workshop (*kitabkhana*) may have taken part in creating the embroidery design. An organic fusion of the aesthetic traditions of Iran, China, and Central Asia distinguish the art of the Timurid period. Reminiscences of Chinese art can be seen in the refined design of the ribbon band and in the use of feathers as an embroidery material. (Feathers were traditionally utilized to adorn the headdresses of empresses in China into the early twentieth century.) Since almost no artistic textiles from the Timurid period are found in museum collections around the world, this work from the Kremlin Museums is truly one of a kind.

Another rare artifact is a helmet with a mask (cat. 8) that is linked to ancient traditions of nomadic culture and most likely dates to the Timurid period in Iranian history. It completely covers the warrior's face and repeats anatomical features, with openings cut for the eyes, nostrils, and mouth. The helmet's functional purpose is skillfully combined with its decoration of a floral design that enlivens the entire surface.

While sources documenting the arrival of these two Timurid items in the treasury of the Russian tsars have yet to come to light, most of the Iranian objects from the sixteenth and seventeenth centuries entered Russia as diplomatic gifts. State relations between Russia and Iran are usually thought to have begun somewhat earlier, that is, around the second half of the fifteenth century.

According to Ambrogio Contarini, the Venetian ambassador to Uzunkhasan (khan of the Turkmen tribe Aq Qoyunlu, who established a new state in Iran), Grand Duke Ivan III of Moscow sent an embassy to Iran in 1474, led by Marco Rufo.[6] The 1580s saw the beginning of regular exchanges of embassies between Russia and Iran. Russian archival documents show that, from the end of the sixteenth century throughout the entire seventeenth century, twenty-nine Iranian embassies visited the Russian state. The two countries' mutual interest was primarily prompted by specific political considerations. All through the sixteenth century and the first third of the seventeenth century Iran and Turkey were embroiled in military conflicts, namely, in a "struggle for sovereignty in the Near East and the Transcaucasia, and for control of the trade routes linking Europe with Asia."[7] The question of trade routes in the southeast territories and the entire "Black Sea–Caucasus" region, which was linked in turn to the security of its southern borders, also played a significant role in Russia's foreign policy. In resolving this question, Russian interests coincided closely with those of Iran. And while an anti-Ottoman alliance that included Russia was not in fact created, friendly relations of mutual benefit were preserved between Russia and Iran. Grigory Kotoshikhin, the undersecretary of the Ambassadorial Office, wrote in the mid-seventeenth century, "We do not wage war with the Persian sovereign. . . ."[8]

Also central to Russo-Iranian contacts in the sixteenth and seventeenth centuries were mutually beneficial trade interests. The importance of a Russo-Iranian trade route was obvious not

FIGURE 3. *Remembered as Ivan the Terrible, Tsar Ivan IV was a contemporary of shahs Tahmsap and Isma'il II in Safavid Iran and sultans Süleyman the Magnificent and Selim II in Ottoman Turkey (Kremlin Museums, inv. no. Zh-1912).*

only for commercial exchanges between the two neighboring countries but also for European and Asian trade in general. Already in the fifteenth century merchants from western Europe attempted to organize transit routes through the south of Russia into Iran and India, thereby establishing a new trade route that could compete with those already in existence. This was the goal of Contarini's embassy, for example. With the annexation in the mid-sixteenth century of the entire Volga basin into the Muscovite state, this route became much more profitable, secure, and economical than the traditional Asia Minor route. European traders also noted the advantage of the Volga route. The Swede Johann Kilburger wrote in 1673, "Persian trade is far more convenient and this route could also be used to traverse Russia with less danger and provide Eastern goods to Europeans."[9] Johan de Rodes, a Swede who lived in Moscow from 1650 to 1655 and made a special study of Russia's domestic and foreign trade policies, noted, "It is much better for the Persians to buy through Russia than to receive [goods] through Ormuz."[10] From the first half of the seventeenth century the Russian state began to act as an intermediary between Iran and Europe, re-exporting to European countries the raw silk that the developing European textile industry so urgently needed. Kotoshikhin wrote, "The tsar himself traded with Persian traders in silk, both raw and processed, and in all kinds of Persian goods."[11]

Throughout the seventeenth century the Russian state pursued a firm policy towards western European traders with the aim of protecting the interests of its own merchants, yet it also encouraged trading by Eastern and especially Iranian merchants. As scholars of Russia's economic situation in the seventeenth century have noted, "Eastern merchants were not subjected to territorial limitations. Customs tariffs were eased somewhat for them."[12] According to the Trade Agreement of 1667, as the charter issued by Tsar Alexei Mikhailovich on 31 May 1667 was called, the right of a monopoly on transporting goods from Iran, particularly raw silk to western European countries, was granted to the Iranian trading company New Julfa, located in a suburb of Isfahan.[13] Russo-Iranian trading contacts in the mid-seventeenth century became so important that a special Persian house (*persidsky dvor*) was established in Moscow expressly for trading goods from Iran.

Use of the Volga-Caspian trade route and trade with Russia were of major importance to Iran. A well-trodden trading route ran through Gilan on the southern shore of the Caspian Sea, then through Shemakh, Astrakhan, and then on up the Volga to Moscow. Diplomatic missions from the shah followed this same road from Iran to Europe. It was not unusual to find in the same caravan one embassy traveling to Russia and another to the countries of western Europe. In 1600, for example, along with the embassy of Pir Quli Beg, bound for Moscow, was an embassy heading to eight European states: to the German emperor, the queen of England, the kings of Scotland, Spain, France, and Poland, the pope in Rome, and the doge of Venice. This embassy was led by Bayat Husayn Ali Beg and the Englishman Sir Anthony Shirley, who had been in the service of Shah Abbas I for several years.[14] The embassy included in its number Uruj Beg, a nephew of the ambassador. He subsequently stayed in Europe, converted to Catholicism, and is best known by the sobriquet Don Juan of Persia.[15] Russian ambassadors to the countries of western Europe also frequently performed diplomatic missions for the Iranian state. In 1588, for instance, a Russian courier to the German emperor brought a document from the shah of Iran as well as documents from the Russian tsar.[16]

Wares imported from Iran in the sixteenth and seventeenth centuries included arms and armor, items to adorn horses, and decorative fabrics. Among them was the celebrated shield created by Muhammad Mumin (cat. 5). This masterpiece of international importance was forged from a single sheet of watered steel. The entire surface of the shield is ornamented with damascened motifs, and the use of different gold alloys makes the motifs particularly noteworthy. The subjects depicted and the way they are executed parallel the work of Iranian miniaturists in the second half of the sixteenth century. This exceptional shield entered the Tsar's Treasury as part of the "escheated" property of Prince Fedor Ivanovich Mstislavsky, who died in 1622 without heirs, and it became one of the chief components of the so-called Grand Attire, the main set of ceremonial armor that the tsar wore in his role as military commander. Mstislavsky was a member of one of the most illustrious and ancient princely lines in Russia and a renowned military leader during the reign of Ivan the Terrible (fig. 3). In addition, he was considered one of the real pretenders to the Russian throne after the death of Fedor Ivanovich, the last tsar of the Rurik dynasty. Also a pretender to the role of Russian tsarina was Prince Fedor Mstislavsky's sister, Irina Mstislavskaya. When Tsar Fedor Ivanovich's marriage to Tsarina Irina Godunova failed to produce children, a group of boyars close to the tsar contemplated replacing her with Prince Fedor Mstislavsky's sister. The conspiracy failed, and Irina Mstislavskaya was removed to the Ascension (Voznesensky) Convent in the Moscow Kremlin, where she lived in seclusion until her death.

This same meticulous craftsmanship and splendid artistry distinguish other pieces of Iranian arms and armor that were brought to the court of the Muscovite tsars, including a broadsword and saber with scabbards (cat. 12, 13) and a ceremonial mace (cat. 14). They reveal Iranian armorers were skilled at a wide variety of metalworking techniques, such as gold and silver inlay, engraving, openwork carving, and embossing, as well as creating lavish combinations of precious stones. With the technique of inlay they attained the precise delineation of the design against the contrasting ground. With engraving they emphasized a fantastic play of light and shade, and with openwork carving they achieved a sense of depth.

To a distinct category of Iranian art belong those works made of gold or those mounted in gold and adorned with precious stones. These include the dagger presented by the Iranian merchant Muhammad Qasim in 1617 (cat. 15), the staff given to Patriarch Filaret in 1629 (cat. 17), the bridle from the embassy of 1641 (cat. 18), and the buffalo horn in a gold mount presented to Tsar Alexei Mikhailovich by the embassy of the Dutch Republic in 1665 (cat. 16). Also in this group are two royal thrones — the first presented by Ambassador Lachin Beg in 1604 (Kremlin Museums, inv. no. R-28) and the second associated, legend has it, with gifts presented to Tsar Ivan the Terrible and later restored for Tsar Mikhail Fedorovich (Kremlin Museums, inv. no. R-29) — and two saddles presented in 1589/1590 and 1635 (Kremlin Museums, inv. nos. K-209, K-210).

All these objects of Iranian art share a number of stylistic and technological features. The mounts contain a very high gold content of 900 and 985, and selected rubies, tourmalines, turquoises, and pearls are arranged identically. Most of the works are decorated with small pieces of green glass. The same method was used throughout to mount the precious stones. Medium-sized stones are set in low-relief mounts that are molded to the shape of the stone. For larger stones the mounts are more three-dimensional and shaped like flat flower petals. Small stones, pearls cut in half, and green glasses are set in smooth round mounts or elongated bezels that mimic the shape of a slanted leaf. The treatment of the golden surfaces — embossed and then lightly chased — is the same in this group of objects. Curved stems bear distinctive swelling leaves, buds, five-petaled flowers, and stylized lotus blossoms, creating an asymmetrical design that flows freely across the surface. A border or trim of tiny stones and glasses emphasizes the silhouettes of the objects or their principal functional elements. Each color scheme is refined and noble, with the saturated color of the precious stones strikingly offset by the restrained pattern of the gold ground. Such a preponderance of similar features suggests a single center of production

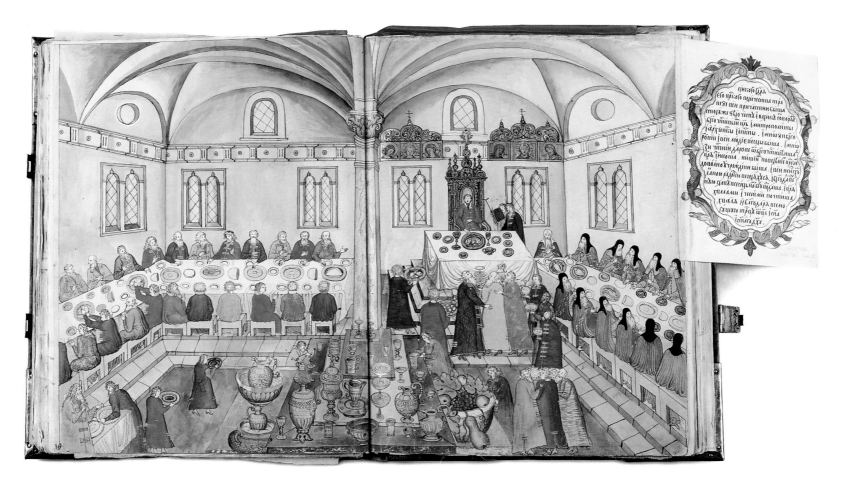

FIGURE 4. *The tsar was the focus of attention at banquets held in the Reception Hall of the Palace of Facets, as seen in this* Book on the Selection to the Most High Throne of the Great Russian Realm of the Great Sovereign, Tsar and Grand Prince Mikhail Fedorovich, Autocrat of All Russia, *Moscow, 1672–1673 (Kremlin Museums, inv. no. Kn-201).*

for the entire group of objects. This center apparently specialized in items made of gold and precious stones with a clearly expressed character, as the surviving pieces demonstrate. It enjoyed an obvious monopoly on the production of gold items, inasmuch as Iran had virtually no local source of gold in the sixteenth and seventeenth centuries, and the metal was most often utilized as imported foreign currency. In all probability the center was a specialized jewelry workshop (*zargarkhana*) that served the court and moved with the shah from capital to capital. In the course of the sixteenth century those cities were Tabriz (from 1502), Qazvin (from 1548), and Isfahan (from 1598). Works of Iranian art made of gold and dating from the Safavid period are extremely rare in museum collections. Even the former shah's collection in Tehran

contains no gold works earlier than the eighteenth century. The group of Iranian gold objects brought to Russia as ambassadorial gifts is thus truly unique.

Splendid examples of Iranian patterned weaving attest to an unprecedented upsurge in the production of the applied arts in Iran during the sixteenth and seventeenth centuries. Particularly cultivated was artistic weaving, which, with its refined decorative sensibility and vibrant color, most fully reflected the artistic characteristics of the era. Iranian textiles are distinguished by their abundant color combinations, their wealth of patterns, and the distinctive rhythm of their composition. The most common motifs associated with the sixteenth and seventeenth centuries were derived from plants and flowers. A whole meadow of flowers—

their buds drooping under their own weight or striving upward and captured there for an instant, twining around each other or standing alone — appears in Iranian textiles of this period. Carnations, irises, hyacinths, narcissus, lilies, and anemones are woven in silks of pure resonant tones. Gold thread, woven into the warp of the fabric, shimmers alternately in the pattern and on the bright ground. The two-dimensional, stylized floral motifs most frequently depict the entire plant, including stem, leaves, flowers, and even the root system. This indication of their real existence is underlined by the detailed elaboration of the plant's individual characteristics and the inclusion of still-life details, such as soil, clouds, tiny birds, animals, and insects.

In addition to fabrics with plant designs, Iranian weavers produced so-called figurative fabrics, which unquestionably became the highest achievement of Iranian artistic weaving. Russo-Iranian diplomatic and trade contacts contributed to the permanent presence of Iranian luxury fabrics in the Tsar's Treasury. Unfortunately, only a small percentage of the enormous quantity of fabrics mentioned in documents of the sixteenth and seventeenth centuries has survived. The inventory of gifts that Shah Abbas II presented to Tsar Alexei Mikhailovich in 1650, for example, listed "over one hundred and seventy pieces of various velvets, both smooth and woven of gold thread, all manner of damasks, satins, eighteen striped gold sashes, nine gold and silver carpets, six colored carpets, one hundred and eleven taffeta pieces from Yazd [*dorogi yasskiye*], seventeen taffeta pieces from Kasan [*dorogi kashanskiye*], and twenty-two taffeta pieces of novelty [*dorogi novogo dela*]." [17]

Iranian fabrics woven with floral ornamentation were occasionally made into saddlecloths in Russia and used during the tsar's ceremonial processions. Also of great interest is the hanging woven with the lion of St. Mark, the coat of arms of the Republic of Venice (cat. 9). Obviously produced by Iranian weavers for export, the hanging inexplicably found its way into the treasury of the Russian tsars in the seventeenth century. Another group of Iranian embroidered objects includes a horse's caparison (*cheprak*), one of the numerous items (according to archival documents) presented by the embassy of Hasan Aga in 1644 (cat. 11).

The cover for the tsar's throne was constructed from pieces of two Iranian carpets with pairs of embroidered peacocks, fish, lions, and mythological *ch'i lin* (cat. 4). Iranian artists appropriated these motifs, originally symbols of good fortune, from the repertoire of Chinese designs in the Timurid period. This continual exchange of cultural traditions among diverse peoples, which began in the medieval period and eventually found its way to Iran in the decades that followed, was expressed in the active reworking and creative rethinking of elements from Chinese design, such as lotus flowers, clouds, the *chi* serpentine ribbon motif, and fantastic animals. Though stylistically close to the Kasan pile carpets from the fifteenth to seventeenth century, the embroidered carpets used in Russia for making this special cover must be dated to the seventeenth century. Supporting this argument is the method of embroidery utilized, which is similar to an entire group of Iranian embroidered items in the museums' collection that is linked to the ambassadorial gifts of 1644. Distinguishing characteristics include the use of thick cotton thread for the couching and an identical method of securing the gold and silk threads, called *klopets* in Russian.

All of the Iranian works in the Kremlin collection share an unusual purity of style. The overall selection of ornamental motifs and schemas, with the entire surface covered with swirling designs or curving stems and the pattern divided into strips or medallions, is evident in the decoration of arms and armor, artistic textiles, and metal works alike. Together they represent the finest examples of Iranian art from the sixteenth and seventeenth centuries, and not surprisingly they occupy a place of honor in the treasury of the Russian tsars.

DIPLOMATIC AND TRADE LINKS between Russia and Turkey were established almost immediately after the formation of the Turkish state, with its capital in Istanbul, at the end of the fifteenth century. In response to an inquiry sent to Moscow with a representative of the Crimean khan, Grand Duke Ivan III directed the embassy of Mikhail Pleshcheev to the Turkish sultan Bayezid II in 1489. Permanent diplomatic and trade contacts between Russia and Turkey are traditionally thought to have been established in 1495. Russian archival documents of the sixteenth and seventeenth centuries make mention of the many Turkish envoys and merchants that traveled to the Russian court. The archives of the Ambassadorial Office indicate Turkish envoys visited Moscow in 1522, 1525, 1570, 1577, and 1593. [18] In 1522 the Turkish ambassador Iskander Beg presented a document from the sultan granting Russian merchants freedom to trade in the territories of the Ottoman Empire. Turkish embassies frequently counted among their numbers representatives of the Orthodox patriarchates and episcopates that came within the purview of the Turkish state in the fifteenth through seventeenth centuries. In turn, Turkish merchants took advantage of every opportunity to bring their goods to Russia, and almost always they were part of the embassies of Orthodox representatives. For example, Turkish merchants accompanied Patriarch Jeremiah of Constantinople on his visit to Moscow.[19] In addition, the ethnic origins of envoys and merchants from Turkey were quite diverse and often included the scions of illustrious Greek families.

Russo-Turkish diplomatic and trade relations were interrupted in the first decade of the seventeenth century during Russia's Time of Troubles, with its interregnum, foreign intervention, and internal wars. Contacts between the two countries were renewed and placed on a more permanent footing after the accession to the throne in 1613 of Tsar Mikhail Fedorovich Romanov, whose reign began a new dynasty (fig. 1). Thomas (Foma) Cantacuzene, the Turkish ambassador to Moscow, led several embassies to Russia (1621, 1624, 1627, and 1630, among others).[20] Also known are the 1631 embassy of Mustafa Mehmed Aga,[21] the 1642 embassy of Kizil Geush,[22] and the 1645 embassy of Mustafa Arsalan,[23] all of them Turkish merchants (fig. 4).

Given the extremely complex international situation in Europe, the Mediterranean, and western Asia at this time, the Russian state was necessarily flexible in its relations with Turkey. Until the end of the seventeenth century the Russian state did not join any of the anti-Ottoman alliances that were formed in Europe and Iran, even though this was a diplomatic goal for many European nations. No direct military conflicts occurred between the two countries during the entire sixteenth century and up until the mid-seventeenth century, with the exception of a failed attempt by the Turks to take Astrakhan in 1569.

The history of Turkey has been intimately linked with that of countries in the Near and Middle East, North Africa, and the Balkans. The art and traditions of those peoples that composed the newly formed Ottoman Empire exerted an enormous influence on cultural life. By the end of the fifteenth century the reworking of these traditions produced a unified decorative and figurative system of Turkish art. Its distinguishing characteristics were a powerful decorative impulse and a style of ornamentation that soon reached perfection. Most Turkish applied art from this period emphasized a multilayered composition that fostered a process of gradual perception intended to unfold in precise stages. Moreover, the surface of objects or individual details of the pattern were covered with a delicate design of plant motifs and geometric forms that are visible only at close range. Among the most widely used plant motifs were tulips, carnations, dog roses, hyacinths, and pomegranate fruits and flowers, all treated in a manner close to their botanical prototypes. Tulips and carnations were regarded with the greatest affection. Their forebears, growing wild in the steppes and mountain regions, at one time figured in the folk art of the Turkic tribes.

The most distinctive characteristics of Turkish applied art in the sixteenth and seventeenth centuries were vividly displayed in those forms, especially weaving, the production of arms and armor and ceremonial horse harnesses, and jewelsmithing, that had long been developed in Asia Minor and were directly connected to ceremonial occasions at the sultan's court. Characterized by large, bold patterns and vivid colors, the earliest Turkish fabrics in the treasury of the Russian tsars date from the second half of the sixteenth century. Fabrics from an earlier period, along with many other Turkish objects, most likely perished during one of the frequent fires that ravaged Moscow in the fifteenth and sixteenth centuries and often inflicted irreparable losses on the Kremlin Treasury. Particularly shattering was the Moscow fire of 1547, in which the Tsar's Treasury and the depository of the Kremlin workshops were destroyed.

Dated to the reigns of Tsar Ivan the Terrible and Sultan Süleyman the Magnificent is a white-and-gold satin with a pattern of large tulips arranged vertically on curving stems. Today several pieces of this fabric, though uneven in shape, have been preserved in a seventeenth-century caparison from the Stable Treasury (cat. 22). Even a cursory examination reveals the outlines of the fabric pieces are those of secular clothing. Quite likely the saddlecloth was made from one of Ivan the Terrible's numerous robes that had been sewn from fabric brought to the court by the Turkish merchant Mustafa Çelebi. The prudent reuse of Turkish fabrics at the Muscovite court was a regular occurrence, prompted by the high cost of imported textiles and the desire to preserve examples of great artistic value.

Turkish textiles were often incorporated into the so-called *khoromnyi nariad,* sets of items used to decorate state apartments for everyday use and on ceremonial occasions. These include the large hanging that served as a room partition in the tsar's private apartments (cat. 28). Window and door openings were draped with smaller hangings. Pillow covers and similar goods constituted an important part of Turkish weaving production in the sixteenth and seventeenth centuries and were sold on both the domestic and foreign markets. One pillow cover, listed as such in the 1687 inventory of the Armory, was used in Moscow as a central element of the tsar's ceremonial *saadak,* a case for a bow and a quiver with arrows that was solemnly carried during his inspection of troops (cat. 30).[24] Iranian gold brocaded velvet woven with gold thread makes up the border. Combining fabrics of different designs and from different countries in a single object was a common practice in medieval Russia, where domestic production of luxury fabrics began only in the eighteenth century.

The Muscovite state found immediate use for the marvelous examples of Turkish arms and armor it received. In the sixteenth century sets of Turkish armor and battle equipment outfitted the central unit of the Russian army, the gentry militia cavalry. Even in the seventeenth century, when Russia increasingly relied upon the military expertise of progressive western European states to arm itself, Turkish arms and armor remained in use. Numerous examples of Turkish edged weapons (those not involving gunpowder or explosives) and armor became part of the Muscovite court's ceremonial accouterments.

One Turkish helmet (cat. 21) worn by the tsar during ceremonial military reviews acquired the local name of *erikhonskaya shapka* (adorned or elegant helmet), a description applied to others of similar shape and decoration. Afanasei Pronchishchev, the Russian ambassador to Turkey, brought the helmet to Russia in 1633, and Tsar Alexei Mikhailovich wore it on his military campaign of 1654–1656. Tsar Mikhail Fedorovich, the father of Alexei Mikhailovich, owned a Turkish *iushman* (cat. 20), a chain-mail shirt with a series of square metal plates inserted into the mesh. Such armor not only served a utilitarian military function, but it was also an essential part of the military garb worn during official court ceremonies.

Practically every kind of Turkish edged weapon, including sabers, broadswords, and daggers, is represented in the treasury of the Russian tsars. Their hilts are generally made of gold or gilded silver adorned with incised or niello foliate designs. Precious stones, turquoises set in tall mounts, and nephrite plaques with damascening heighten the decorative effect. Among the finest examples of this type of weapon is a seventeenth-century Turkish saber (cat. 24). Recorded in the 1687 inventory of the Armory as a saber of the Grand Attire, it is listed as number one, evidence of its exceptionally high status among ceremonial arms.

Artisans in Ottoman Turkey were extremely open to other cultures and were willing to utilize their best achievements (fig 5). An indication of this is a dagger from the imperial collection of weaponry (cat. 23). Its grip and sheath are made of nephrite inlaid with gold and precious stones, a technique associated with Turkish art in the sixteenth and seventeenth centuries. A vivid enamel pattern featuring a selection of floral motifs typical of Turkish art embellishes the back of the dagger's guard. The blade is the work

FIGURE 6. *In this posthumous portrait from the mid-nineteenth century, Tsar Alexei Mikhailovich holds the scepter and orb, symbols of imperial authority. He ruled Russia from 1645 to 1676 (Kremlin Museums, inv. no. 1961).*

of the armorer Mahmud, son of Mas'ud, an Iranian craftsman who inscribed his name on the surface of the watered steel.

Among the items with a precise date of acquisition by the Treasury is a *shestoper,* or mace, that was brought to the court of Tsar Alexei Mikhailovich by Dmitry Astafiev, a Greek merchant from Istanbul, in 1656 (cat. 26). Originally a formidable weapon, this mace is made of gold, set with rubies and emeralds, and decorated with green and white enamel. Unquestionably it belongs among the ceremonial objects that the Russian tsars regarded as attributes of imperial power (fig. 6).

In terms of the magnificence of their decoration, many works made by Turkish armorers come close to being genuine masterpieces of the jeweler's art. Judging by their high professional standards and meticulous execution, the variety and complexity of techniques used, and the rich materials utilized, numerous items that found their way into the arsenal of the Russian tsars were the work of armorers and jewelers who were closely associated with the court workshops of Istanbul. Craftsmen of the most diverse specializations, from armorers, goldsmiths, and engravers to bone and stone carvers, were employed in these ateliers.

Also attributable to court workshops in Istanbul are a large number of ceremonial horse harnesses that were brought to the court of the Russian rulers. In Turkey, as in Russia during the sixteenth and seventeenth centuries, ceremonial processions were highlights of official court events. Such processions were similar in both countries, from their precise regimentation and the large numbers of people who escorted the ruler, to the beauty and sumptuousness of the garments worn by the participants and the luxurious horse accouterments, including caparisons sewn with pearls and precious stones. Indeed, items of ceremonial horse attire were often included in the ambassadorial and trade gifts from Istanbul (cat. 31). A large group of valuable horse adornments was among the gifts presented by two Greek merchants from Istanbul, Avram Rodionov and Dmitry Konstantinov, in 1656. These gifts may well have included a luxurious saddle adorned with gold plaques set with rubies and emeralds framed in seed pearls (cat. 32). The matching bridle and chest strap, decorated with magnificent silver-gilt chased plaques set with nephrite, turquoise, and pearls, may have been brought to Moscow at an earlier time, perhaps during the embassy of 1621 headed by Thomas Cantacuzene (cat. 35, 36 and fig. 7). Highly prized beyond the borders of the Ottoman Empire, such Turkish horse accouterments figured prominently among the items brought to Moscow by representatives of other countries. Thus, in 1625 Ambassador Rusan Beg of Iran presented Tsar

Mikhail Fedorovich with a gift from Shah Abbas I: a harness set with gold plaques ornamented with a fine niello foliate motif and large semiprecious green stones called peridots in Russian documents (cat. 39–41).

Turkish harnesses, like many other items of Ottoman workmanship, were often decorated with costly plaques made of gold and gems or of semiprecious stones with damascening and chips of precious stones. The former type was produced in different sizes and in the most fantastic shapes: tulips and carnations, pomegranate fruits, various leaves and buds, and many-pointed stars. As a rule their edges were embellished with openwork that could be combined to form a variety of plant designs. Decorated on the front with precious stones and multicolored enamel, the underside frequently featured a carved pattern of flowers within a mesh of pointed ovals, a design also found in Turkish fabrics. Ottoman jewelsmithing and metal inlay demonstrate the most diverse use of precious stones, with diamonds, rubies, and emeralds beveled in small flat facets around the edges.

Techniques for working with semiprecious stones were well known in Turkey and had a long history in the territories that made up the Ottoman Empire. In the sixteenth and seventeenth centuries the quality of the craft developed and improved, as did various other trends in Turkish art. The decoration of items created from nephrite, amber, rock crystal, and/or lazurite became truly magnificent. Entire surfaces were covered with inlays of gold and colorful gems set in patterns consisting of the traditional motifs of tulips, pomegranate fruits, and stems bearing many-petaled flowers. Gold wire that formed linear designs as well as the tiny pieces of gold leaf used to delineate leaves and petals were thin enough to allow for shallow incisions in the stone beneath. The resulting visual effect of fine lines of damascening enlivened with gems resembled a costly decorative fabric.

The principal group of Turkish jeweled items in the treasury of the Russian tsars can be attributed to workshops active in Istanbul. According to Russian archives, the capital of the Turkish state, traditionally called Tsargrad in Russia, was acknowledged as both the place where luxury wares were produced and the departure point from which they were dispatched. Among them were items decorated with semiprecious stones, such as the squat spherical nephrite bowl that the Greek merchant Georgios Panagiotis brought to the court of Tsar Mikhail Fedorovich in 1632 (cat. 42); the crystal tankard that Patriarch Cyril I Lukaris of Constantinople offered to the Muscovite court that same year (cat. 43); a scent bottle for rose water presented in 1656 (cat. 47); and a lazurite writing set (cat. 48). The application of

FIGURE 7. *Sultan Osman II may have presented a chest strap (detail above) and its accompanying bridle to Tsar Mikhail Fedorovich in 1621. Made of gold, silver, rubies, pearls, turquoise, and nephrite, it is an exceptional example of Ottoman artistry (see cat. 36).*

translucent, red, and green enamel, complemented by a specific selection of gems, creates an all-over carpetlike pattern that gives the impression of extraordinary wealth and magnificence. Another noteworthy object is the gold pocket watch with a calendar, the mechanism of which was made in Geneva and its case in Istanbul (cat. 49).

Other works possibly attributable to Istanbul jewelers are the gold plaques depicting four-cornered crosses that are called panagias in Russian documents (cat. 64, 65). The production of objects bearing Christian motifs was not uncommon in the history of the Ottoman Empire. Ottoman sultans ruled over peoples representing more than sixty major ethnic groups and three of the world's monotheistic religions: Islam, Christianity, and Judaism.[25] Moreover, the percentage of Christians among the general population of the Ottoman Empire was very high. According to the testimony of Cristobal dé Villalón, who was taken prisoner by the Turks in 1552 and became the personal physician of Sultan Süleyman the Magnificent, Istanbul contained more than forty thousand Christian households,

compared with sixty thousand Muslim ones.[26] Located in the outskirts of the city was the court of the patriarch of Constantinople, who maintained connections with the entire Orthodox world. Presumably those centers of production that traditionally made items intended for this large Orthodox population, as well as for sale in Russia and neighboring Christian states, continued to function within the framework of the Ottoman Empire. Thus, textiles with designs of crosses, cherubim, and even detailed Orthodox scenes were frequently found among Turkish ambassadorial and trade goods presented to the Muscovite court. Two such fabrics were used to make the sakkos of Patriarch Iosif, a contemporary of tsars Mikhail Fedorovich and Alexei Mikhailovich (cat. 62 and fig. 8). The gold fabric that constitutes the body of the vestment — patterned with four-pointed crosses, the monogram of Christ, and cherubim — was recorded among the items brought from Istanbul by the Russian ambassadors Afanasei Pronchishchev and Tikhon Ermolov in 1633. The front of the sakkos is light blue satin with a woven image of Christ enthroned — and it is the very fabric from which was made the sakkos of Metropolitan Dionisii, the former head of the Russian church during the reign of Ivan the Terrible. Recent investigations have proved the fabric for Metropolitan Dionisii's garment was woven in the court workshops of Istanbul in the last quarter of the sixteenth century.[27] Quite possibly other Turkish fabrics with Orthodox motifs that were brought to Moscow were woven in the same ateliers. Such fabrics probably amounted to just a small part of Turkey's extensive textile production, and only a few examples today remain in the world's museums. Only the museums of the Moscow Kremlin have preserved an entire collection of them.

Goods made by Turkish craftsmen not only became a vital part of the official and daily life of the Moscow court, but they also exerted a profound influence on the activities of the Kremlin's own craftsmen. For instance, frequent references are made in the inventories of the Armory to this or that weapon being prepared "in the Turkish manner" or decorated similar to "Turkish work." Armguards made by the celebrated Russian armorer Nikita Davydov, who worked for several decades in the Armory Chamber, are one example of this (cat. 57). Hints of Turkish art are evident in the decoration of the saber of the Grand Attire (cat. 56), which was made in the Kremlin in the late 1620s and early 1630s for Tsar Mikhail Fedorovich. Russian silver wares of the second half of the seventeenth century are embellished "with Turkish niello," an intricate plant design typically found on many works as a supplemental decorative element.

FIGURE 8. *Patriarch Iosif served as the head of the Russian Orthodox Church in the mid-seventeenth century. The satin body and front panel of his sakkos, with images of Christ enthroned, were woven in Turkey. The embroidery was added in Moscow after 1658 (see cat. 62).*

Brought in large quantities from Istanbul, gold plaques set with gems adorned many items intended for secular and church decoration, such as the gold tabernacle from the Annunciation Cathedral of the Moscow Kremlin (cat. 63), which was probably created by jewelers of the Gold Chamber of the Kremlin workshops, and the ceremonial saddle made by craftsmen of the Stable Office (cat. 55). Many jeweled plaques produced in Moscow were based on Turkish prototypes. One example is part of a set of decorated gold plaques (*kruzhivo*) adorning a robe that was given to the Kremlin jewelers for the purpose of copying it. "By order of the great sovereign tsar Mikhail Fedorovich . . . a whole link was taken from the *kruzhivo* of the tsar's robe as a model. . . ."[28]

Artists' copies of patterns from Turkish fabrics are often found in Russian ornamental embroidery. Examples include the *saadak* with large carnations embroidered on red velvet (cat. 60) as well as the yoke and cuffs on the sakkos of Patriarch Iosif (cat. 62) that are made of black velvet and decorated with gold embroidery to resemble a Turkish textile. In both cases the Russian embroidery is worked in gold thread. This predominance of gold thread in Russian embroideries, even those modeled on multicolored fabrics, was not accidental. The color range of gold and silver embroidery imparted a greater sense of solemnity and ceremonial effect than did the original fabric. While such opulent decoration might seem quite inappropriate today, it kept well within Russian aesthetic ideals of the seventeenth century.

Preserved over several centuries in the Moscow Kremlin, the Eastern collections of the tsars testify to how Russians increasingly came into contact with the cultures of diverse peoples and states. These ambassadorial and trade presentations exemplify the peaceful, productive exchanges that occurred between peoples of different faiths and traditions. Today this collection confirms the Kremlin Museums' role as an historical treasure house of both Russian art and art from abroad, and specifically that of the East. Precisely dated and of the highest artistic quality, these works represent significant stages in the history of Iranian and Turkish art. Many of them were created in important centers of production, if not in workshops attached to the imperial court. Of unique artistic value are gold objects crafted by Iranian artists who worked for the shah, splendid items made by jewelers in Istanbul, and textiles with Christian motifs. In addition, those items that have been restored by museum specialists and given new attributions stand as testament to the attention and care with which members of the professional staff of the Moscow Kremlin approach the historical and artistic treasures of the East that are in their care and are an integral part of the world's cultural heritage.

Russian-Iranian Relations
in the Mid-seventeenth Century

Rudi Matthee

Diplomatic relations between Safavid Iran and Russia go back to 1521, when Shah Isma`il sent an envoy to Muscovy (Moscow). For the next half century, official contacts between the two states remained limited to a few desultory attempts by Isma`il's successor, Shah Tahmasp, to convince Tsar Ivan IV to take Iran's side in his struggle against the Ottomans.[1] There is no evidence that the tsar reciprocated by sending diplomatic envoys to Iran. Relations intensified during the first part of the reign of Shah Abbas I in the late sixteenth century, but they tapered off following the onset of Russia's so-called Time of Troubles in 1598 and remained low key during the next fifteen years of famine, disease, and disorder. They picked up

again with the accession of the Romanov dynasty in 1613. Russia long remained weak, unstable, and impoverished, and efforts at forging diplomatic ties never regained their former level of intensity.

Most Iranian embassies were commercial missions in disguise, consisting of diplomats doubling as tax-exempt merchants who transported silk and metalwares to Moscow and returned with Russian furs and falcons. Every meeting included an exchange of gifts, the sine qua non of early modern diplomacy. Persian-language sources yield little information on the nature, quantity, and value of these offerings, and they do not mention presents going north.[2] None of the artifacts survived the turmoil that gripped Iran following the fall of the Safavids in the early eighteenth century. Most of what is known about the exchange comes from Russian-language sources. By contrast, the Kremlin Armory in Moscow holds many gifts that originated in Isfahan, including ceremonial arms and armor, jewelry and objects inlaid with precious stones, and textiles, from fragments of silk to beautifully woven garments.[3]

Even if trade superseded them in importance, political issues always formed a vital part of the exchange between Iran

and Russia. Shah Abbas in particular was keen to persuade the Russians to join him in an anti-Ottoman coalition. Of more immediate concern to the Iranians was control over Georgia. As the object of their southward thrust into the Caucasus, Russians had been building frontier fortresses in the region since the mid-sixteenth century. The tsar also showed an interest in Iran as a potential partner against the Ottomans. In addition, Moscow further sought to keep unruly tribes away from its southern border and to secure the safety of trade routes connecting Iran and Europe.[4]

After the death of Shah Abbas I in 1629, the nature of this interaction changed. Shah Safi I, his successor, proved to be less interested in building an anti-Ottoman coalition, especially after he concluded a lasting peace with Istanbul in 1639. State involvement in trade also decreased when Shah Safi abandoned the silk-export monopoly that his predecessor had granted to Armenian merchants operating in Iran. This policy of benign neglect continued under Shah Abbas II, who oversaw a period of relative stability. Only a few Safavid missions seem to have visited Moscow in these decades.

The Russians meanwhile faced numerous problems, including the Nikonian Schism within the Russian Orthodox Church. Most importantly, the country became embroiled in a war with Poland, which caused it to seek closer ties to the Ottomans. Desirous to keep marauding tribal peoples (Kalmyks, Nogay, and Lezghis) in its southern borderland in check, Moscow nevertheless sent nine missions to Iran from 1647 to 1662—three major (*velikie*) embassies and six minor (*legkie*) ones. Worried about Iran's strategic designs, Russian envoys were keen to consolidate their country's influence in the Caucasus. Central to this regard was the territory of Georgia, the eastern half of which had been a vassal state of Iran since the early seventeenth century.[5] Over time Georgia's rulers sought to replace Safavid overlordship with Russian protection. Tsar Alexei Mikhailovich sent several envoys to Isfahan requesting the shah to prevent the Lezghis from lending support to the Crimean Tatars, to refrain from assisting the Uzbegs, or to punish the khan of Shamakhi for meddling in the affairs of Daghistan and threatening the governor of Astrakhan.[6]

The Iranians, in turn, accused Moscow of making common cause with tribal leaders and building fortresses in the Caucasus. In the 1640s the Russians constructed a fort on the Terek River in support of Taymuraz, the ruler of Georgia who had turned to them for assistance after being deposed by the Iranians. It took several Russian missions to put this issue to rest. In the process Safavid forces led by the khan of Shamakhi destroyed the fortress.[7] The Russian envoy who visited Isfahan in 1654 is likely to have been Lebanov-Rostovsky. Accompanied by two hundred people and two hundred camel loads of brandy, precious furs, and other rarities, he was charged with proposals to solve the conflict as well for negotiations about silk.[8] In response, Shah Abbas II sent Khandan Quli Sultan to Moscow. Nothing is known about a mandate and its results.[9] By the time Ambassador Miloslavsky was dispatched to Isfahan in 1662, Cossack depredation along the Caspian Sea had joined the list of Iranian complaints about the Russians.[10]

The Russian embassy that arrived in Isfahan in the summer of 1664 stands out for its size—its entourage numbered three hundred fifty people, although one source claims it was eight hundred—as well as for the historical pattern it followed and the information still available. The Russians requested free trade in the shah's realm. Wealthy merchants in the mission's entourage brought rich presents, including coaches, horses, exotic animals, and a great many precious furs.[11] Despite these grand gifts, the suite was poorly received in Isfahan. Iranians had long considered the Russians to be unclean, primitive, and perpetually drunk. They called them the Uzbegs of Europe, in the words of the Frenchman Jean Chardin.[12] One Safavid chronicle speaks of *Rus-i manhus*, ominous Russia, a term that over time came to be used routinely for Russians.[13] With their meager gifts and their requests for loans, the envoys who had visited Isfahan during the Time of Troubles had only reinforced Russia's image as a bedraggled country. Breaking with their habitual hospitality, the Iranians had often treated Russian envoys accordingly, to the point of forcing them to approach the shah on foot.[14]

After an initially friendly reception, matters turned sour at the time of the official audience, when the presents were officially submitted to the shah. Soldiers blocked the entranceways to the royal square leading to the palace, forcing the Russian visitors to leave their horses and walk the remaining distance. When they refused to dismount, the Russians were forcibly pulled off their horses and brought before the shah. Their presents were shown only after darkness had fallen. This humiliating incident was apparently too much for the leader of the mission: he died a few days later.[15]

Chardin attributes the shabby treatment to Iranian disgust with the filthiness of the Russians and the realization that they were just merchants in disguise who were trying to benefit from tax-free trade. The Dutch add several more compelling reasons for the discomfiture, explaining that the shah had blown up in anger upon learning that, instead of building a trading post, the Russians intended to erect a fortress along the Caspian Sea. He is said to have blamed the Russians for instigating Cossack raids in the area. A final cause of royal displeasure was a claim to the tsar's right to take control of Georgia following his son's marriage to a daughter of the Georgian ruler.[16] The poor reception had long-term repercussions as well, for it may have prompted Tsar Alexei Mikhailovich to encourage the Cossacks to invade Iran after the death of Shah Abbas II in 1666.[17]

This same period saw an increasingly important role for semiprivate trade in bilateral relations that involved members of Iran's Armenian community. Armenian merchants operated out of New Julfa, the suburb of Isfahan where Shah Abbas I had settled them. At this time the Julfans were exploring routes to Europe beyond the hazardous Ottoman one and the oceanic connection that had been opened by European maritime companies. Worsening conditions for minorities in Iran also prompted

FIGURE 10. *Opulence and emblems of authority were hallmarks of gifts presented to foreign rulers. This pouncing lion appears on a link of a silver-gilded horse chain created in the workshops of the Moscow Kremlin (see cat. 52).*

wealthy Julfans to seek closer ties to the outside world as a way of investing in the future. This explains the exceedingly rich presents that Zakharia Shahrimanean carried on behalf of his father, Sarhad, on a trade mission to Moscow. Serving as a royal merchant for both Shah Sulayman and Grand Vizier Shaykh Ali Khan, Zakharia brought with him the so-called diamond throne, made of silver and studded with diamonds and other precious stones. Valued at eighty thousand gold ducats, the throne was presented to Tsar Alexei Mikhailovich in hopes of gaining trade privileges, most notably an exclusive Armenian right to travel through his domain. Zakharia also planned to strengthen political ties between the Julfan merchants and the Russian crown, with the obvious intent of buying potential protection against the Safavid regime.[18]

The Russians eventually complied, motivated by financial as well as strategic considerations, and offered the Armenians special transit rights in 1667. They hoped for expanded trade that would fill up their treasury. That same year the Treaty of Andrusovo ended the state of war between Russia and Poland and invigorated interest in an anti-Ottoman coalition that might include Iran. The new Safavid ruler, Shah Sulayman, however, proved unwilling to break his peace agreement with Istanbul, and commercial implications took on far greater importance in shaping diplomatic and trade relations for generations.[19]

the golden horde

1. ICON OF THE MOTHER OF GOD GALAKTOTROPHOUSA

Painting: Moscow, 16th century;
oklad: repoussé, Golden Horde or Russia, 14th century;
plaques, Russia, late 14th–early 15th century;
crowns, Moscow, late 14th–early 15th century
Gold, silver, pearls, precious stones, wood

This icon of the Mother of God Galaktotrophousa is a sixteenth-century copy of the Barlovskaya Mother of God, one of the most venerated icons in the Cathedral of the Annunciation of the Moscow Kremlin. Its metal cover (*oklad*) at one time adorned that ancient miracle-working image, which has not survived. The icon's gold *oklad* consists of two crowns set with precious stones, a repoussé (*basma*) ground, and repoussé borders ornamented with fourteen silver-gilt plaques containing the enameled images of two archangels and the Twelve Apostles.

Based on the treatment of the precious stones set in tall arched mounts framed with a fluted band, the crowns of the Mother of God and Christ can be attributed to Russian craftsmen of the late fourteenth and early fifteenth centuries. The plaques depicting archangels and apostles can be dated to the same period on stylistic grounds.

The central motif of the repoussé pattern is a lotus-shaped flower, the so-called Arabian flower that is characteristic of ornamentation in works from the Near and Middle East as well as Central Asia. It also appears in the metalwork of the Golden Horde, where fan-shaped flowers such as those featured on the *oklad* of this icon are found. The pattern on the repoussé borders consists of medallions in the form of smoothed quatrefoils and half-ovals placed crosswise, on which the word "Allah," written in Naskh script, is embossed repeatedly. This repoussé pattern has direct comparisons in the works of craftsmen from the Golden Horde. The *oklad* reflects the artistic connections that existed between early Rus and the cities of the Volga region and the Crimea. It is difficult to determine where the repoussé metal sheets of the *oklad* were produced. Most likely they were made in Moscow with the participation of Golden Horde craftsmen. The image itself, though painted in Moscow by a Russian artist, has its iconographic prototypes in fourteenth-century Italian painting. This work is thus a distinctive symbiosis of the cultures of Russia, the West, and the East.

21

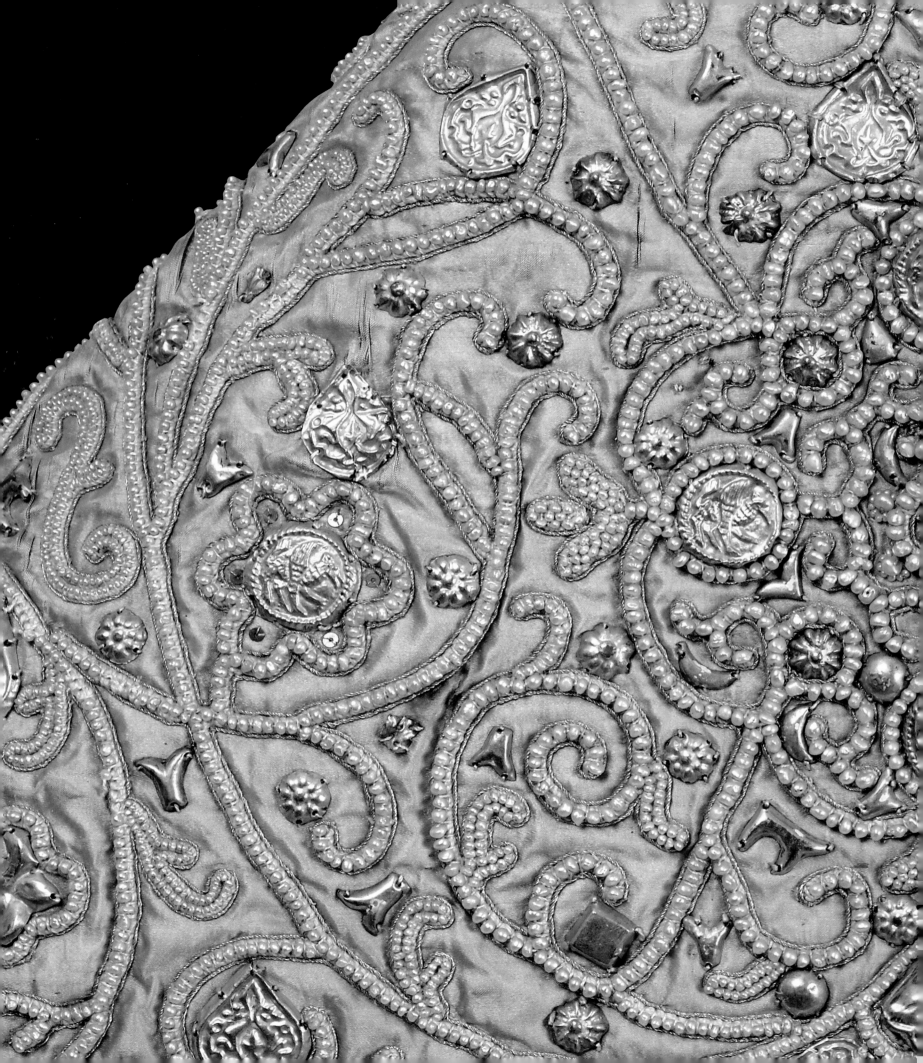

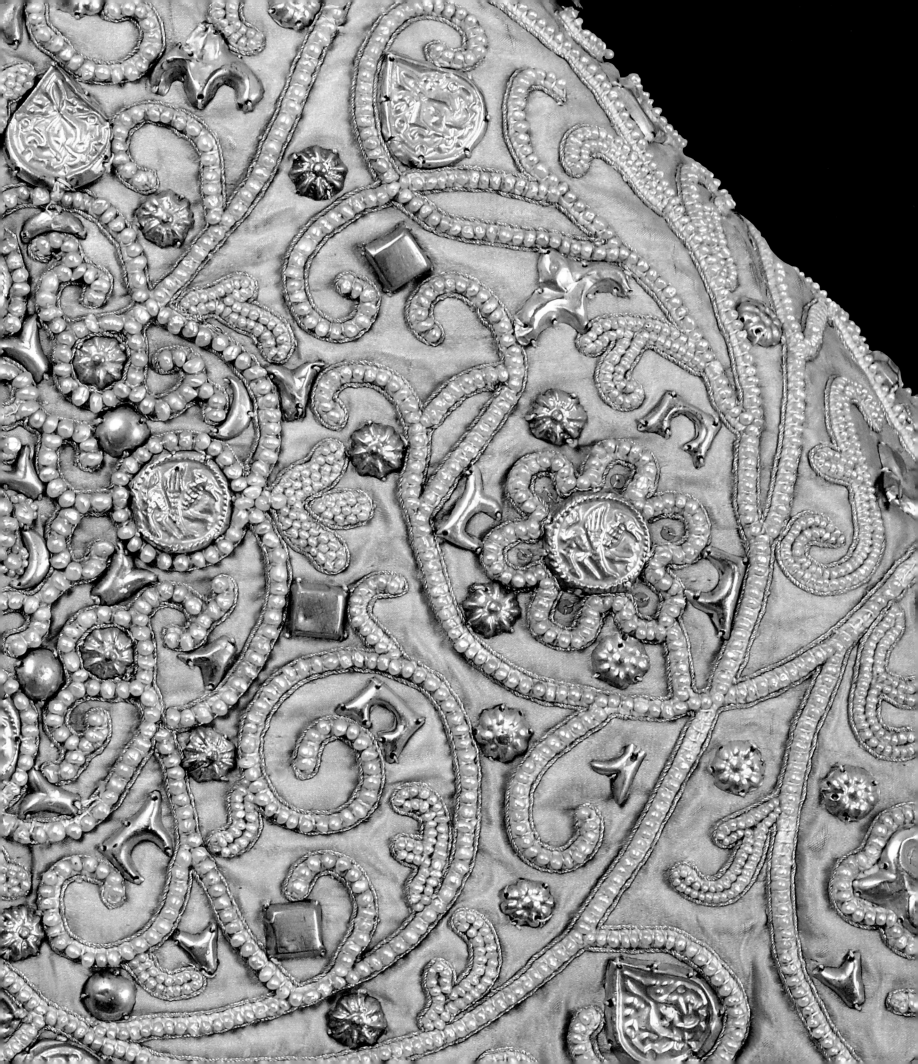

2. PHELONION

Gilded satin: territories of the Ottoman Empire, Damascus (?), 16th century;
sewing: Russia, mid-16th century; plaques: Golden Horde, 14th century, Moscow, 16th–17th century
Gilded satin, satin, sackcloth, silver, gold thread, pearls, copper

Cut like a sleeveless cloak, a phelonion is the outer vestment that an Orthodox priest wears over other garments during the liturgy. Exactly when the phelonion was adopted in the Eastern church is not known, but this style of garment most likely served as the first Christian liturgical vestment. The word appears for the first time in Paul's Second Letter to Timothy: "The cloak that I left at Troas with Carpus, when thou comest, bring with thee" (Tim. 4:13). Early phelonia were bell shaped and of equal length front and back. Particularly emphasized are mandatory elements of the vestment, such as the yoke, hem, cross, and custodia, which symbolize events in the life of Christ. The yoke signifies the marks of Christ's flagellation; the hem represents the road Christ traveled as he was led to judgment. The image on the upper back beneath the yoke recalls the cross that Christ bore on his back to Golgotha. Beneath it, the custodia refers to the star of Bethlehem and the stone that sealed the tomb in which Christ's body was placed.

This particular phelonion is cut in the ancient bell shape. Gold-figured satin with an ornamental design of leaf scrolls and birds woven in gold threads (now badly worn) on a red ground make up the body. Intertwining scrolls form an all-over ogee pattern. In each ogee is a medallion with a figured edge and a floal rosette at its center. The yoke consists of plain pink satin decorated with pearl embroidery embellished with small repoussé plaques of various shapes (see previous page). The four-point cross is sewn entirely of pearls, with small plaques at the center and at each point. Pearl scrolls are embroidered at the corners of the custodia, which is in the shape of a rhomboid of pink satin. The hem is made of plain green satin.

According to legend, this phelonion, like another preserved in the Kremlin Museums (inv. no. TK-2435), was donated to the Protection of the Virgin (Pokrovsky) Convent in Suzdal by Tsar Ivan the Terrible.[1] From time immemorial such donations were regarded as acts that pleased God and thus were an obligatory part of an Orthodox person's religious life. Moreover, the Pokrovsky Convent frequently accepted female members of the royal family as nuns and therefore regularly received royal donations and contributions.

This phelonion has been restored several times. The pearl embroidery, which in execution is typical of the mid-sixteenth century and has many parallels in work from the reign of Ivan the Terrible, apparently was transferred to a new pink satin ground in the seventeenth century. Midsized pearls strung on a single thread and sewn in a pattern of slender stems with shoots and distinctive "whiskers" delineate the embroidery. The tips of the stems bear stylized rosettes and buds. Numerous small silver plaques of various shapes, both smooth and chased, are embedded in the embroidery. The smooth plaques include those in the shape of stylized Chinese clouds, while the chased ones feature images of a *senmurv* (dragon), which served as the coat of arms of the Kazan khanate that formed part of the Russian state in the sixteenth through nineteenth centuries. Today it is incorporated into the coat of arms of the city of Kazan. Undoubtedly made by craftsmen of the Golden Horde, these plaques can be dated to the fourteenth century. The cloud-shaped plaques are similar in ornamentation to the sakkos of Metropolitan Alexei. According to fourteenth-century Russian sources, the khan's wife Taidula, in gratitude for being cured of blindness, gave the metropolitan a vestment ("priestly garments") and a seal ring (see page 3). B. A. Rybakov asserts a fragment of that vestment was preserved in the hem of the sakkos of Metropolitan Alexei now in the collection of the Kremlin Museums (inv. no. TK-1).

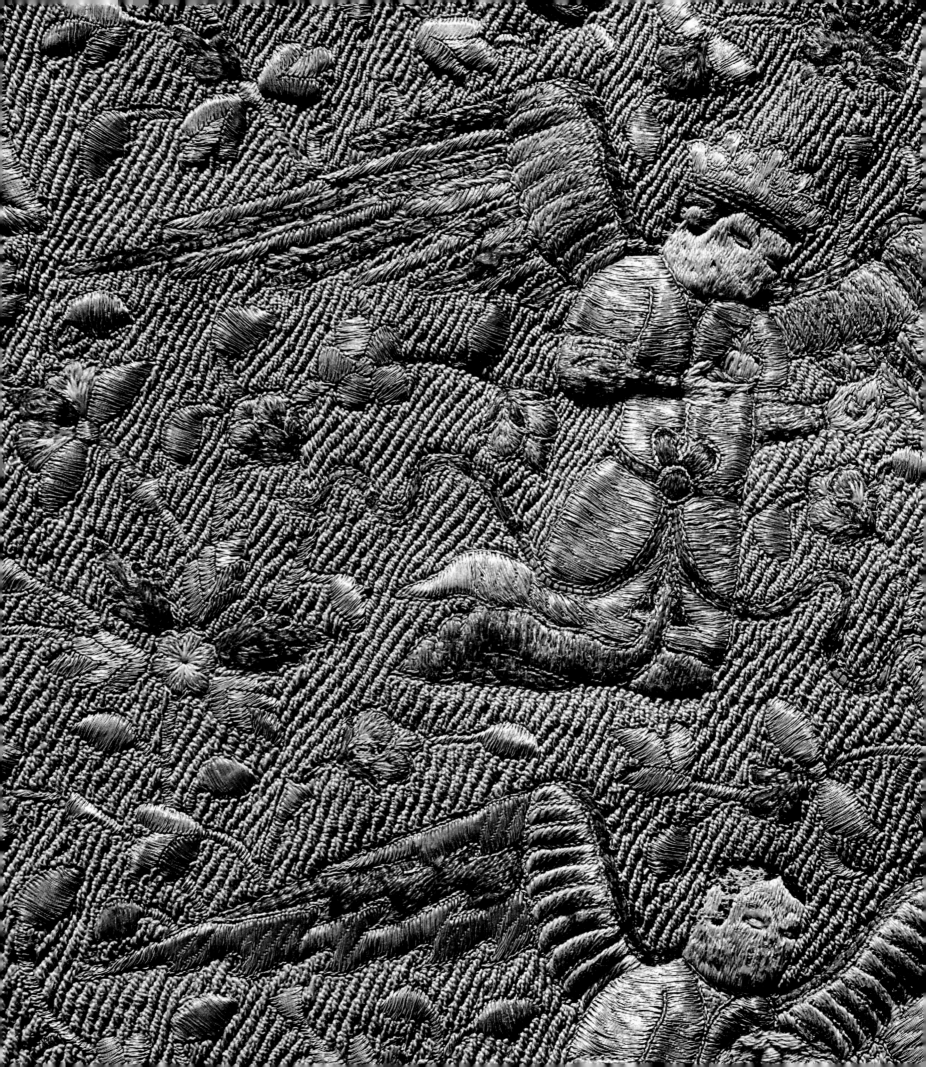

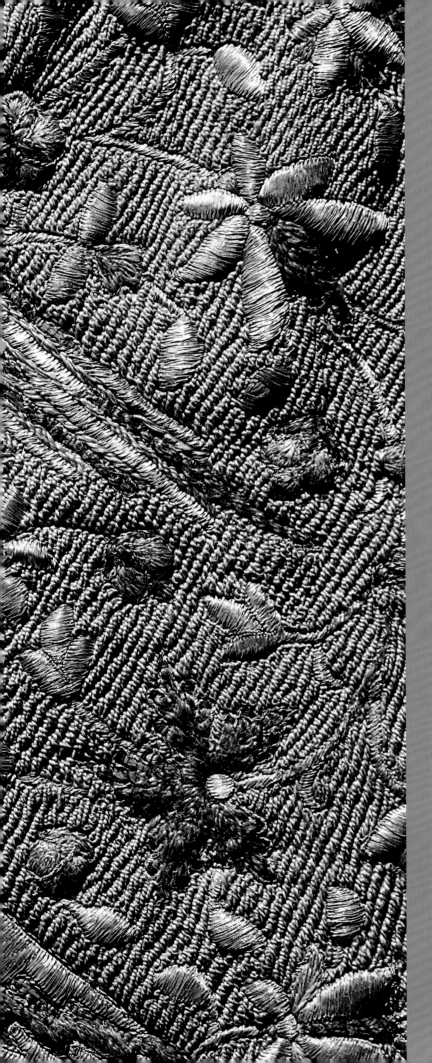

gifts from | IRAN

3. WIDE COLLAR

Iran, 15th century
Silk and cotton fabrics, spun gold and silver threads,
silk thread

In the museum inventory of 1808, this object is listed as an *opush* (cloud collar), with the notation that in earlier inventories it was called "lace."[2] This early Russian term referred to a particular kind of decorative embroidery that was applied to the edges and hem of a garment made for the tsar. In subsequent museum registers the piece acquired its current designation as a wide collar (*opleche*), which is now generally accepted. Other archival documents describe it as being made of "Chinese silk material" or "thick Chinese serge."[3] The collar's Iranian origin had been convincingly proven by the end of the nineteenth century,[4] while a more recent article narrowed the date down to the fifteenth century as the period in which it was created.[5]

The shaped piece consists of a yoke surrounding the collar, straight bands running the length of the front, and a partially preserved hem in the form of a rectangular strip. Across the shoulders, on the back, and in front of the collar are scalloped projections that are described in museum inventories as *gorodki* (turret-shaped ornaments). The scallop on the back ends in a medallion in the shape of a half-palmette.

Embroidered all over the ground of the collar is a pattern of slender scrolling branches with buds, flowers, tiny leaves, and larger leaves worked in green silk, fine-spun gold thread, colored silks, and dark blue "bird-of-paradise" feathers. Each projection of the collar contains two pairs of angels (peris) wearing robes and headdresses and holding plates or vases. Linked directly with the notion of an earthly paradise, this symbolic imagery has a particular mystical significance that is intensified by the use of pure gold thread for the embroidery.

Recent visual examination of the collar has established several stages in its sojourn in Russia, with each one accompanied by major repairs. It has been possible to determine that the original embroidery, stitched with spun gold thread, was executed on a ground of scarlet silk. Preserved on the edges of the collar are quite small fragments of blue silk from the garment to which it was initially attached. This garment was undoubtedly a type of straight-cut Eastern robe without fastenings or collar. The collar's current condition, with its ground embroidered entirely in green silk thread, can be traced in the museums' inventories to the late seventeenth century, when it most likely underwent extensive restoration. Moreover, the extremely faded ground was "couched" with green twisted silk threads in a slanted stitch to imitate the weave of serge. This method of reinforcing caused the compilers of the museums' inventories in the eighteenth and nineteenth centuries to assume that the background was of "green serge." The strongest evidence of these restorations is the presence of a second layer of cotton on the other side to which the green threads of the ground were attached. Repairs were also made to the embroidery itself. Threads of spun silver, now deeply tarnished, were added in those areas where the spun gold thread was lost. Areas of loss in the embroidered bird feathers were filled in with threads of dark and light blue silk.

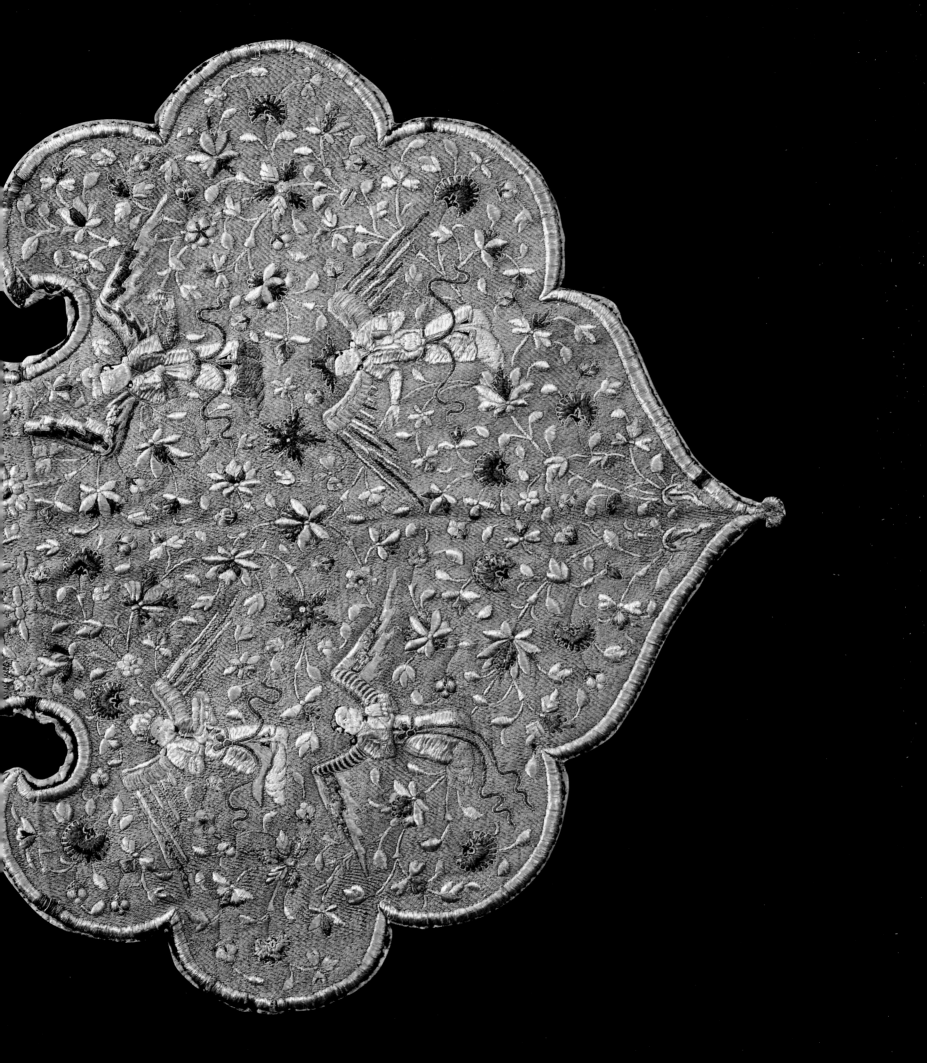

4. COVERLET FOR THE TSAR'S THRONE

Embroidery: Iran, first half 17th century;
execution: Moscow, Kremlin workshops, 17th century
Velvet, canvas, gold thread, silk thread, naboika

Foreign visitors to Russia in the sixteenth and seventeenth centuries often commented on the Russians' love of "covering and concealing everything" as a local peculiarity. All honored objects used for ceremonial purposes were draped with specially prepared covers and cloths.

This coverlet for the tsar's seat (possibly a throne or a portable chair) is made from fragments of two embroidered carpets, which were frequently among the goods brought from Iran. They take the form of an elongated rectangle with two side panels. The central section consists of a carpet with a ground of crimson velvet and a pattern of medallions, while the side panels are constructed from pieces of the border of another carpet, the ground of which is embroidered with gold threads that are now well worn. The embroidery is couched in a regular geometric pattern using thick bundles of cotton and silk threads of various colors and spun gold threads.

A large embroidered medallion in the center is formed by an undulating vine with decorative flowers and leaves. Embroidered inside it are the squat figures of lions pacing towards the center, with stylized cypresses between them. Peacocks face each other, their tails spread wide, in each of the four twists of the medallion. The entire background field is filled with individual stylized trees along with two tulips emerging from the same clump of soil. The corner bosses, also marked by a vine with flowers and leaves, contain designs of individual leaves of various shapes and pairs of peacocks, small lions, and goats. Brown silk outlines define the embroidery, which was stitched in sand-colored, light blue, yellow, and black silks.

The border on the upper and lower edges of the central section and the two side panels is made from the border of another carpet. Gray embroidery fills the entire ground on which are placed plant motifs and individual medallions sewn with dark blue or red threads. The blue medallions contain the figure of a *ch'i lin*, a Chinese mythological animal that here has tongues of fire on its belly, while the red medallions display a pair of fish.

In terms of composition and pattern, both embroidered carpets are similar to a group of pile carpets produced throughout the sixteenth and seventeenth centuries in the town of Kasan. Possibly this is the source of the carpets from which this special coverlet for the tsar's throne was created in the Armory workshops.

The brown *naboika* (block-print fabric) lining has a pattern of small elongated paisley buds that are called "cucumbers" in Russia. Plain woven cottons and prints are known to have been used as packaging material for transporting valuable Iranian fabrics and carpets to Moscow.

In the museums' inventory since the late nineteenth century, this work was included in the section headed "coverlets and scraps left over from the tsar's furnishings." A note attached to the description characterizes it as "the earliest coverlet for the tsar's throne, dating to the fifteenth century."[6] Stylistic and technological analysis of the Iranian embroidered carpets from which this coverlet was made place its production at a later time, perhaps in the first half of the seventeenth century.

5. SHIELD

Iran (Qazvin?), 16th century; master: Muhammad Mumin
Watered steel, gold, rubies, pearls, turquoise, fabric, fringe

Inlaid in gold in a figured border on the rim are the name of the maker of this magnificent shield — Muhammad Mumin — and his occupation as *zernishan* (inlayer). The terse inscription indicates neither the place nor the time in which this true masterpiece of the armorer's art was created.

Forged from a single sheet of watered steel, the shield's entire surface is chased with spiral bands that create the impression of a dynamic vortex. Each alternating band is inlaid with gold. Decorative motifs and figures are based on fairy tales, poems, and legends. Human figures, shown in battle or at the hunt, are set against a ground of trees and flowers and are delineated with a refinement characteristic of sixteenth-century Persian manuscript painting (see frontispiece). Expressive figures on one of the bands depict a moment of furious fighting during a battle, with the result that the friezelike composition successfully conveys the tension of the scene.

If European armorers generally chose scenes and heroic figures borrowed from classical mythology to decorate their knightly armor and rondache shields, Iranian craftsmen, as here, turned to familiar literary heroes. Lions, tigers, leopards, camels, bears, hyenas, gazelles, foxes, and hares further enliven the shield's round surface. In some places combinations of individual animals are incorporated into a general scene, such as and a mountain goat being tormented by predators. Shown on one band is a fantastic bird, a Chinese motif that symbolizes the power of the empress. It is also frequently found in Iranian art. The scenes alternate with bands decorated with the *chi* cloud ornament.[7]

Crisply incised silhouettes of people and animals as well as the surrounding designs are executed in two colors of gold. The main outline is picked out with pure reddish gold, while the details — turban, belt, saber, animals' horns, and so on — are rendered in a greenish gold (an alloy of gold and silver). This imparts a particularly refined tonality that enhances the motif's legibility and adds an element of color. Edging set with rubies and turquoise further adorn the shield. The central one was originally topped with a gold knob, but it was lost by the early nineteenth century.[8]

In addition to its technical sophistication, the shield has an interesting history. It appears to have come to Russia in the second half of the sixteenth century. Initially it belonged to Prince Fedor Ivanovich

Mstislavsky, one of the most prominent political and military figures of the late sixteenth and early seventeenth centuries. A scion of the Gedimin dynasty — he was the son of Prince Ivan Fedorovich and grandson of Prince Fedor Mikhailovich Mstislavsky — he became a boyar in 1576 and was one of the most important landowners in the Russian state. After Tsar Fedor Ivanovich died without an heir, the prince was considered a possible pretender to the Russian throne. In 1604 and 1605 he commanded the troops that Tsar Boris Godunov sent against the first "False" Dmitry. He was wounded in battle near Novgorod-Seversky (December 1604) and then claimed victory over the troops of the pretender near Dobrynichy (January 1605), but he was soon summoned to Moscow by the tsar.

Mstislavsky's political clout and broad connections helped him not only to survive the reign of "False" Dmitry I but also to maintain his position as the head of the Boyar Duma, an advisory council of prominent noblemen. He was entrusted with arranging the ceremonial reception of the future tsarina Marina Mnishek. One of the witnesses to this meeting, the Swedish observer Petr Petrey, made particular note of Mstislavsky's role: "The most distinguished prince and boyar in the country, Fedor Ivanovich Mstislavsky appeared with two hundred other distinguished boyars and princes. . . ."[9] In 1606, however, he was an active participant in the conspiracy against "False" Dmitry I. With the fall of Tsar Vasily Shuisky in 1610, Mstislavsky headed the so-called Rule of the Seven Boyars (*semiboiarshchina*) and took part in drafting an agreement on the selection of Prince Vladislav, son of the Polish king Sigismund III, as Russian tsar. Three years later, in 1613, he was once more considered as a possible pretender to the throne. In describing Mstislavsky, the Dutch observer Isaac Massa wrote, "He was always a devout man and his services were made use of in all wars, as were those of his father before him. Boris [Godunov] was always looking for ways to ruin him, for this is how he liked to punish men of high birth, but he could find nothing to hold against him, so blameless and frugal was his way of life, for his lackeys lived better than he did. However, Boris forbade him to marry so that he should have no heirs, and he died childless. . . ."[10] After Mstislavsky's death in 1622 a portion of his property, including this shield, went to the Tsar's Treasury, where it became part of the Grand Attire of Tsar Mikhail Fedorovich.

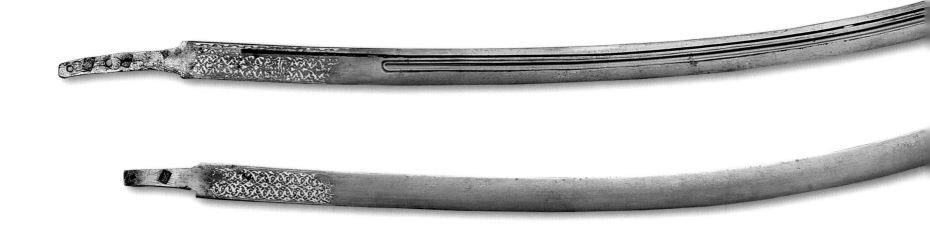

6, 7. SABER BLADES

Iran, Isfahan, first half 17th century;
master: Rajab-Ali Isfahani
Watered steel, gold

Blades made by Iranian swordsmiths were extremely popular throughout Russian history. Forged of Iran's famous watered steel, such blades were prized for their strength, their superior qualities in battle, and their beauty. The surface of the blades was generally inlaid or inscribed with gold.

According to the Arabic inscriptions inlaid in gold and the hallmarks, these two blades from the Armory collection were made by the Iranian master Rajab-Ali Isfahani. One blade was given to Tsar Alexei Mikhailovich in 1675 by Muhammad Husayn Beg, the ambassador of the Iranian shah. The other was presented to the tsar on 11 February 1664 by an Iranian merchant whose name unfortunately has not been preserved.

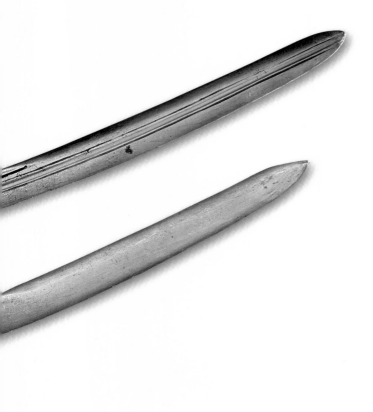

8. HELMET WITH MASK

Iran, 16th century
Steel

The ancient tradition of making helmets with masks that resemble faces extends to the Roman Empire. Examples have been found in the arsenals of nomads across the steppes of the Black Sea region and in the countries of the Near East. Even so, this helmet is extremely rare.

An engraved floral design enlivens the entire surface of the helmet. In addition to a decorative strap, it has a figured top with openings. An Arabic inscription, originally gilded, reads "Merciful, Creator. Most pure, Master, Refuge of the world" and is engraved with exceptional precision.[11] The attached mask entirely covers the face, with features rendered with great realism — note the eyebrows and moustache — and with openings for the eyes, nostrils, and mouth. Ornamental designs are engraved on the cheeks and chin of the mask, and a figured semicircular plate is attached between the brows.

Three similar helmets are listed in the nineteenth-century inventory of the Armory.[12] Today two of them are preserved in the Kremlin Museums' collection, and the third (inv. no. 4406) was transferred to the St. Petersburg Artillery Museum in 1873.

An almost identical iron mask, although without the helmet, is in Dr. Nasser D. Khalili's collection of Islamic works of art. The author of that collection's catalogue, David Alexander, dates the mask to the fifteenth century on the basis of extensive visual evidence, such as the nature of the ornamentation and depictions of warriors wearing similar headgear.[13]

9. HANGING
Iran, mid-17th century
Brocade

The hanging is constructed from two pieces of brocade, each with an identical pattern placed in mirror image. In the center of each piece is an oval medallion filled with flowers. Flanking it on either side are two winged lions that hold shields with the inscription PAX TIBI MARCE EVANGELISTA MEUS, the coat of arms of the Republic of Venice. Surrounding these images are individual tulips, irises, dog roses, carnations, burdock, and thistles. The plants resemble botanical prototypes, with stems, leaves, flowers, and small clumps of soil placed in airy, elegant arrangements and rendered in realistic shades of light and dark blue, pink, and green. Darker tones of silk outline the motifs. The lions are woven of spun silver, with their wings of green, light blue, pink, and dark blue silk, and the inscription on the shields is of black silk. The ground of the central section is composed of fine gold thread, and the border of silver thread has an undulating stem of flowers. The lining is of green taffeta. Individual woven sections are unusually wide (128 cm), which suggests they were produced on double looms.

A similar hanging that also bears an inscription is in the collection of the Kremlim Museums (inv. no. TK-608). In the center, surrounded by a floral pattern, is the coat of arms of the Russian state: the double-headed eagle with triple crowns. Both hangings are listed in the 1706 inventory of the Stable Treasury,[14] which confirms they were produced prior to this date. Their arrival at the Muscovite court can be dated at least as early as the second half of the seventeenth century. Evidence of this is the distinctive method of adding a thick gold fringe to decorate the border, as was done with the hanging with the double-headed eagle.[15] Many objects from the second half of the seventeenth century in the Stable Treasury have with this type of fringe.

Both hangings are interesting examples of Iranian weaving techniques and recall carpet weaving in the articulation of the border and central section. A similar composition distinguishes other hangings and one-piece woven items. This evidently explains why the covering with the lion of St. Mark has been generally described as a hanging.[16] Its mirrored symmetry and particularities of its construction, however, suggest the piece was intended to function as a coverlet. For that purpose it was essential the pattern on the sides should match.

The attribution of these textiles to the late sixteenth and early seventeenth centuries also deserves attention.[17] The depiction and style of the plants resemble Iranian textiles produced in the seventeenth century. Closely based on botanical originals and appearing to grow freely, similar tulips, dog roses, carnations, and thistles are woven into a velvet hanging now in the collection of the Cincinnati Art Museum[18] and are on the silk fabric of a dalmatic now in the Victoria and Albert Museum.[19] Common to all these works are the almost graphic reproduction of the plants and the distinctive delineation of outlines with a more intense shade of silk.

On the basis of these parallels, the covering can be securely dated to the seventeenth century. A more precise date emerges from an analysis of one of the covers. Its Russian coat of arms takes the form of the double-headed eagle beneath three crowns, but the third crown was not adopted until 1625, following the decree of Mikhail Fedorovich in February of that year.[20] On that basis the production of both coverlets should be dated to the middle (not earlier than the second quarter) of the seventeenth century.

The history of how both hangings came into the Tsar's Treasury and the reason for their commission from Iran remain unclear.

10. SADDLE BLANKET

Russia, Kremlin workshops, 17th century;
velvet centerpiece: Iran, early 17th century;
damask border: Italy, 17th century
Taffeta, velvet, silk

As part of a horse's parade trappings, such blankets were often formed from imported luxury fabrics that were kept in the Tsar's Treasury and distributed as needed.

The central section of this blanket is made of embossed gilded velvet from Iran. Bunches of flowers on long slender stems, arranged in an elegant flowing rhythm and drooping under the weight of the flower heads, create an attractive pattern. This naturalistic treatment contrasts with the clearly stylized rendering of the flowers themselves and the purely decorative way in which they are arranged. Distinctive features include the forms of the bands on the stems. Although the weave's repeat pattern does not coincide with the design, it nevertheless produces an elegant interweaving of the overall piece. The vivid color scheme is now noticeably faded. Dyestuffs used in Iranian textiles in the seventeenth century yielded a great variety of colors that unfortunately were often fugitive.

The border of the saddle blanket is made of Italian gilded satin with a large stylized plant design. Combining fabrics made in different places into a single item was typical of Russian court life.

11. CAPARISON

Iran, early 17th century; additions: Moscow,
Kremlin workshops, 17th century
Cloth, gold and silk threads

A significant portion of the ambassadorial and trade wares brought into the Muscovite state from Iran and Turkey in the seventeenth century included ceremonial horse trappings, above all parade caparisons. In early Russia such coverings were traditionally the most important component of the trappings worn by horses on ceremonial occasions. All of the parade caparisons were kept in a special area of the Stable Treasury, from where they were distributed for official ceremonies. Caparisons functioned in several ways, and their form varied accordingly. Some covered the chest and croup of the horse; others were draped beneath the saddle, while still others were placed on top of it. A single horse might be decked out with several caparisons at one time.

Documents show that in 1644 Ambassador Hasan-Aga (as the name was written in Russian transliteration) brought several embroidered cloth caparisons from Shah Abbas II of Iran. This one is decorated with embroidery that emphasizes its main functional components — the place for the saddle and a border visible on three sides. A large leaf with serrated edges, flanked by two pacing lions and surrounded with symmetrically placed flowers and stems, fills the middle section. The border on three sides also has a symmetrical design of large denticulate leaves and flowers embroidered in spun gold with small amounts of colored silk. The composition and placement of the embroidered pattern, as well as the decorative treatment of the place where the saddle rests, all indicate the cloth is a *cheprak*, a caparison of a specific cut. Rectangular or trapezoidal in shape, the *cheprak* extended behind the saddle to cover the horse's croup. This particular cloth was widened with a different colored cloth after it came to Russia.

12. BROADSWORD AND SCABBARD

Iran, before 1645
Steel, gold, precious stones, nephrite, velvet, braid

This broadsword is more European than Iranian in decoration and shape. Its straight steel blade is double-edged and has a pronounced flat heel with a shallow channel running the length of each side. A third of the blade's overall length is decorated with gold damascening on a blued ground.

Carved of nephrite, the hilt is encrusted with emeralds and rubies in gold rosette-shaped mounts. A large, faceted emerald is set in the top of the pommel. The gold grip has curved quillons with dragon heads on the tips. The surface of the guard is covered in fine black enamel carved with a stylized plant design, which creates a striking combination of gold and black.

Colored velvet covers the wooden scabbard. The fittings — the mouth, two suspension mounts with loops for a cord, and the chape — are made of gold. Nephrite plates encrusted with gold and precious stones decorate these fittings. The underside is treated in the same style and technique as the hilt. The scabbard still retains a fine silk braid that was used to suspend it from a belt.

This broadsword is an exceptional example of Iranian armory and jewelry. Its small dimensions support the idea that it was intended for a child or adolescent. It cannot be ruled out, however, that it was acquired for the heir to the Russian throne, namely, Tsarevich Alexei Mikhailovich.

According to surviving documents, the broadsword was purchased from the nobleman Semen Volynsky, scion of an ancient and illustrious family. (His ancestor Dmitry Bobrok-Volynsky was considered a hero of the Battle of Kulikovo that was fought against the Golden Horde in 1380.) The family had long since lost its former status at court, and Semen Volynsky occupied no important state or military posts, receiving the title of "Moscow nobleman" only in 1627. From then until 1642 he was appointed to military duties on the southern Russian fortification lines and in the towns of Mosal'sk and Putivl'. On 8 May 1642 Semen Volynsky was a member of an embassy dispatched to Iran. In all likelihood he acquired this broadsword at that time, and it was subsequently purchased from him for the Armory Chamber.

13. SABER AND SCABBARD

Iran, first half 17th century
Steel, wood, gold, silver, jasper, precious stones, braid

This saber (see previous page) is a splendid example of Eastern ceremonial weaponry. Its blade, with its distinctive delicate silvery design on a dark ground, is forged from watered steel. The presence of the famous lion hallmark of the workshops of the Iranian shahs confirms the high quality of the blade. Incised beside the gold mark is an Arabic inscription: "The owner will become famous." The hilt is made of pyrite, a form of dark green jasper with red veining. Its pommel and crosspiece, together with the fittings of the scabbard (mouth, tip, and five clips), are decorated with a mosaic of turquoise, rubies, and emeralds. Gold plaques with tiny faceted diamonds are attached to the center of each scabbard band. The belt matches the costly decoration of the saber: it is woven of fine silver-gilt wire, and the inside is lined with silk braid. Colored enamel, typical of Iranian jewelry work of the mid-seventeenth century, enlivens the springs and hinges of the belt. In the inventory of the Tsar's Field Treasury of 1654/1655, however, this saber is noted as being of Egyptian work.[21]

Tsar Alexei Mikhailovich received this saber on 29 September 1646 from Prince Iakov Kudenetovich Cherkassky, scion of a distinguished Cherkessian family. After he converted to Christianity in 1625, Cherkassky began his service at the court of Tsar Mikhail Fedorovich. During the reign of Tsar Alexei Mikhailovich, Cherkassky attained the highest state offices, overseeing the Russian army's infantry regiments and foreign military specialists. During Russia's war with Poland (1654–1667) Prince Cherkassky was the First Wojewode of the Grand Regiment (that is, the commander in chief of the Russian army). Troops under his command captured the cities of Orsha, Kovno (Kaunas), and Grodno, and on 29 July 1655, after a successful engagement with the great Lithuanian Hetman Janusz Radziwill, captured Vilno (Vilnius), the capital of Lithuania. He served in the same capacity during the unsuccessful siege of Riga in 1656. During the Russian forces' retreat from the city, a rear guard under his command thwarted all attempts by the Swedes to rout the Russian army. He died ten years later, on 8 July 1666.

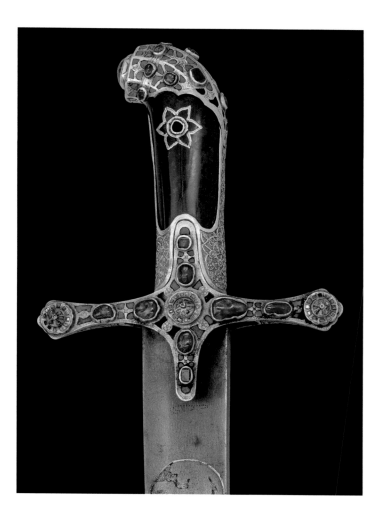

Prince Cherkassky's gift to Alexei Mikhailovich may have been linked to two events: first, his coronation as tsar, and second, the granting to Cherkassky of the highest service rank, that of boyar. Both events took place at the end of 1645. During the coronation ceremony, Prince Cherkassky was "first among his peers" and sat at the tsar's table for the feast in the Faceted Chamber.

The saber received exceptionally high status in the Tsar's Armory. In the inventory book for 1686/1687 it was listed as number two among the sabers of the Grand Attire. It was ranked first in the 1654 inventory of the weapons that Tsar Alexei Mikhailovich took with him on his military campaigns. This saber may well have been displayed on the tsar's saddle during his triumphal entry into Moscow after the capture of Smolensk in the winter of 1655.

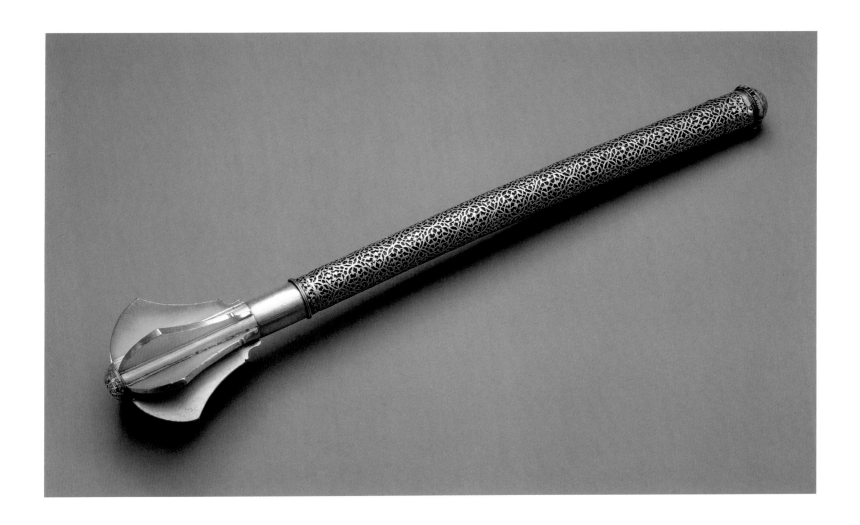

14. CEREMONIAL MACE

Iran, mid-17th century
Gold, wood, turquoise

An offensive weapon, a mace typically has a head made of six or more flanges. The Armory Museum contains this unique mace with seven cast-gold flanges. Its head is 98 percent pure gold and is quite heavy, weighing more than a kilogram. Together with its handle it weighs 1,350 grams. The general visual effect, however, is one of lightness rather than massiveness. This is largely due to the grip, whose wooden base is covered with gold leaf embossed in an unusually complex open-work pattern of slender stems and leaves elegantly intertwined.

The gold mace is associated with Russo-Iranian relations in the mid-seventeenth century. During a ceremonial reception held on 3 February 1658 in the Faceted Chamber of the Moscow Kremlin, the ambassador of Shah Abbas II of Iran presented it to Tsar Alexei Mikhailovich. In the inventory of the Armory dated to the late seventeenth century, the mace was given pride of place among all the maces listed there.

15. DAGGER AND SHEATH

Iran, first half 17th century
Steel, wood, gold, rubies, turquoise, pearls

In the seventeenth century a knife or dagger was an essential component of the Russian tsar's campaign or battle dress. It hung from a belt or sash cinching a long narrow shirt (*chuga*) over which plate or chain-mail armor was worn. This dagger, made by Iranian craftsmen, is one of the few remaining decorated examples of this type of weapon from the Armory Treasury. According to an entry in the income and expenditure book for 1616/1617, it was presented to Tsar Mikhail Fedorovich in 1617 by the Iranian merchant Muhammad Qasim: "Damascus steel knife, sheath and hilt mounted with turquoises and ruby chips, on top of the knife a spinel between pieces of seed pearl . . . humbly presented to the Sovereign by the merchant Muhammad Qasim of Qizilbash Shah Abbas in the previous year."[22]

Since no indication is given in the accession documents that the merchant was acting on behalf of Shah Abbas I, this must have been Qasim's personal gift. The dagger was transferred to the Armory the following year, on 22 September 1618. Throughout the seventeenth century, however, it was not housed in the Armory Treasury but rather in the Artisan Chamber together with items of the Grand Attire, the ceremonial regalia of the Russian autocrats.

The dagger's double-edged blade is forged of watered steel and has four facets. Small in scale, its colorful combination of precious stones creates a dazzling decorative effect. The hilt and sheath are covered in gold with an embossed plant design and a floral motif composed of precious stones, pearls, and turquoise. A large ruby is mounted on the end of the hilt.

16. HORN

*Gift of the States General of the Dutch Republic
to Tsar Alexei Mikhailovich in 1665
Iran, first half 17th century
Buffalo horn, gold, precious and semiprecious stones, glass, enamel*

Topped with a cast form of a man's head, this splendidly polished buffalo horn is decorated with thin sheets of stamped gold set with large turquoise cabochons and small rubies, tourmalines, and glass in gold mounts.

Scholars believe many of the works by Iranian craftsmen in the Armory collection that entered the Tsar's Treasury as gifts share a number of stylistic and technological characteristics. This assertion lends credence to the possibility that these works were produced in the same artistic center, specifically in the court workshops (*karkhana*) of Isfahan.[23] These include the staff presented in 1629 to Patriarch Filaret in the name of Shah Abbas I[24] (cat. 17) and the gold bridle given by Shah Safi to Tsar Mikhail Fedorovich in 1641 (cat. 18). This horn would seem to have been created in Isfahan as well. The precise circumstances under which it made its way to Holland remain unknown, but it has been established the horn left that country in 1664 when the embassy from the States General of the Dutch Republic traveled to Moscow with Jakob Borelius at its head.

The embassy took along a colorful assortment of gifts, including silver goods, spices, fabrics, and works by European artists in stylized Eastern designs, as well as genuine pieces from distant lands. In addition to furniture inlaid with precious woods, Far Eastern porcelain, and lacquerware, the tsar and his court were presented with two "elephant teeth, gilded on the tips and middle with gold leaf" and "a precious unicorn horn in a box, covered with coarse red cloth and lined inside with green velvet." This mythical animal's horn was actually a buffalo horn in a jeweled mount.

17. STAFF

Gift of Shah Abbas I of Iran to Patriarch Filaret in 1629
Iran, late 16th–early 17th century;
additions: Russia, first third 17th century
Wood, gold, precious and semiprecious stones, glass

The staff (*zhezl* or *posokh*) is an essential attribute of the higher clergy. At the culminating moment of his enthronement, the head of the Russian church is solemnly handed the staff that symbolizes his spiritual authority over the faithful.

According to early inventories, the staff presented to Patriarch Filaret is made of cinnabar wood that has been covered with thin plates of fine gold repousséd with a plant design of slender intertwined stems bearing five-petaled flowers, buds, and slanting elongated leaves. Small turquoises in low mounts and large rubies and turquoises in tall ones, chased to resemble flowers at the intersection of the stems, accentuate the design. Other bands of small turquoises emphasize the staff's structure. The ground of the repoussé pattern is worked in flat chasing.

Decorated with the same pattern as the central part of the staff, the upper section of the mount is further embellished with large flowers and several rows of leaves, but it lacks the precious stones. On a plain ground is the eight-pointed cross of Golgotha flanked by a spear and sponge and accompanied by a carved Russian inscription (see left). Since both the mount's decoration and the image are somewhat stiffly executed, they undoubtedly were additions carried out in the workshops of the Moscow Kremlin.

The 1630 inventory of Patriarch Filaret's treasury mentions several alterations to the staff. At one time a broad crosspiece (now lost) was added to the top. This so-called horn was a distinguishing feature of patriarchal staffs. In the commentaries of Metropolitan Savva, who compiled a review of the Patriarchal Sacristy in the nineteenth century, the side elements of the "horn" were derived from the pastoral crooks of the early patriarchs of Constantinople.

18. BRIDLE

Gift of Shah Safi of Iran to Tsar Mikhail Fedorovich in 1641
Iran, first half 17th century
Gold, silver, rubies, emeralds, turquoise, leather

The horse's bridle is ornately embellished with gold designs. Narrow red leather straps edged with small gold rectangular plates as well as plates with a large ruby and four small emerald chips alternate with others set with a central emerald and ruby chips in each corner. A gold crosspiece connects the bridle and the collar, which takes the form of a figured plate with large rubies and emeralds in tall mounts (see left). These are framed by a floral design of small rubies, emeralds, turquoise, and glass, each of which projects from the embossed gold ground worked in flat chasing. Similar designs of five-petaled flowers and long leaves composed of small stones and glass on a repoussé ground worked in flat chasing also ornament the dagger sheath that Muhammad Qasim presented to Tsar Mikhail Fedorovich (cat. 15).

It was previously thought the bridle was among the gifts that Shah Safi offered to Tsar Mikhail Fedorovich in 1635.[25] Recent archival information — with the lengthy title "Book telling of the visit made by ambassador Asan-Bek and merchant Agi Magmetev to the Sovereign bearing an official document and gifts from Shah Safi, notes about their appearance at an audience before the Sovereign, about the ambassador's sudden death soon after and about the assumption of all ambassadorial duties by his brother Savakhan-Bek" — fixed the time of the bridle's acquisition and linked it to gifts of the embassy of 1640–1643.[26] In the document that members of the embassy presented to Tsar Mikhail Fedorovich from Shah Safi, the shah expresses his regret at the demise of Patriarch Filaret and also informs the tsar of compensation given to Russian merchants for the losses they suffered as robbery victims in Gilan.

The official audience took place at court on 22 March 1641. The embassy book for 1640–1643 describes the ceremony at which gifts of thoroughbred horses, gold-mounted saddles, caparisons, fabrics, carpets, and precious vessels were given to the tsar. "They brought gifts into the chamber and set them by the table and they held the Argamak horses in the courtyard on the plank walkway and the Treasury secretaries accepted the gifts and the stable grooms lead away the Argamak horses."[27] After the presentation ceremony servants of the court offices took the gifts to the Tsar's Treasury, while the horses — four stallions and five mares — were escorted to the stables.

Among the gifts was a *mushtuk* (a bridle with a bit) with a chest strap mounted in gold with rubies and emeralds. The value of this gift was set at 155 rubles.[28] The gold harness with rubies and emeralds, small chips, and "tiny elongated turquoises" was listed in the 1706 inventory of the Stable Treasury as number three in the "gold harness" section with the note, "This harness was sent to the Great Sovereign as a gift from the Qizilbash Shah Safi in the year 149 [1641] on the 22nd day of March."[29]

Various names describing bridles can be explained by the fact that horse bridles were differentiated according to the form of the iron mouthpiece: a bridle with a mouthpiece was called a *mushtuk*, one with a straight bit was an *uzda*, and if it lacked an iron bit it was categorized as an *ogolov'e*. By the end of the seventeenth century the iron initially utilized in making the mouthpiece of this bridle was replaced with a bit mounted in silver, which was subsequently lost. Also lost was the chest strap that formed part of the set.

51

19. SADDLE

Russia, Kremlin workshops, second half 17th century;
velvet: Iran, 17th century
Silver, wood, velvet, leather

By the end of the seventeenth century the Stable Treasury contained one hundred fifty saddles made by Russian craftsmen. Almost half of them were *archaki,* saddles with a cushion attached to the seat. Light and comfortable, they were intended for use "in the field," that is, for marches and hunts.

This unique *archak* is covered with embossed Iranian velvet. Its soft, luxurious seat differs from other saddles of similar structure in that it almost completely lacks metal details. Originally no metal frame enclosed the front and back pommels. Instead, according to the 1706 inventory of the Stable Treasury, a gilt braid was used. (It was lost by the end of the nineteenth century.) Only the four buttons that fasten the cushion and the loops on the protruding sections of the saddle's panels are fashioned of gilded silver.

Every component — the wooden framework, the front and back pommels, the leather side panels, and the swansdown cushion — is covered with rare fabric. Woven in relief on a plain silver ground is a pattern of crowns, wreaths, and bouquets of carnation flowers and buds outlined in a fine black contour line. The dominant colors are various shades of gold, straw, and light brown. Although the fabric has lost its initial bright colors, the pale blue, green, and pink shades can still be detected. A network of medallions outlined in black encloses the pattern.

The saddle has two side panels — small round wings with rectangular flaps beneath them — that prevented the stirrup straps from rubbing the horse's flanks and the rider's legs. Leather sections below the wings and the flaps are lined on top with the same velvet and edged with green leather. This marks the first occasion on which the saddle is being exhibited in its fully reconstituted form. When it was shown at exhibitions of Muslim art in Munich (1910) and of art from Iran and Turkey in the Kremlin Museums (1978), the saddle was displayed without the wings because those parts were thought to be lost. Inna Vishnevskaya and Olga Melnikova discovered these missing pieces had been in the museum all along, kept in a separate location as examples of rare luxury fabric. After undergoing examination and restoration by textile conservator Irina Kachanova, the wings were reunited with the saddle.

In addition to this saddle, several other rare saddles of Russian workmanship have survived in the museums' collections. They are decorated with Iranian velvet on which floral designs, carnations, and bouquets of flowers in vases appear on a light straw-colored, light brown, or green ground (Kremlin Museums, inv. nos. K-440, K-473, K-486, K-509, K-516, K-917, K-1122). The velvet covering of these saddles is badly worn and disintegrating, a result not simply of the passage of time but also of frequent use in processions, ambassadorial receptions, and other ceremonies of the imperial court.

gifts from | turkey

20. CHAIN-MAIL SHIRT

Turkey, 17th century
Steel

According to inventories compiled in the nineteenth century, this armor once belonged to Tsar Mikhail Fedorovich. In the seventeenth century protective armor made in the East was highly prized and put to practical use as helmets, armguards, *zertsala* (four or more large steel plates joined by rings or straps), and *kol'chugi* (shorter chain-mail shirts).

An *iushman* is a piece of armor that has rectangular plates inserted into the chain mesh. Unlike the *kol'chuga*, the *iushman* has a front opening that allows it to be donned like a jacket. This form of protective armor appeared in the Near East and Central Asia in the late fourteenth century and was used in Russia and eastern Europe to the end of the seventeenth century.

The plates of the *iushman* generally protected the wearer from the most dangerous blows to the stomach. In more heavily reinforced examples, such as this one made by Turkish craftsmen,

the plates also covered the warrior's chest, sides, and back. Twenty rectangular plates are interwoven on the chest. When the *iushman* is strapped on, eight of them are covered by other plates. Fifty-four smaller plates protect the back, and each side section is covered by thirteen more plates. Arabic inscriptions are damascened in gold in an ornamental frame on each plate. On the top layer of plates in the front are inscribed the words, "Glory to you throughout the whole world." Inscriptions on the back plates are heavily worn, but the words "merciful, creator" can be deciphered on some of them. Attached to the lower plates is a wide mesh hem.

In the inventory book of 1686/1687 this *iushman* is listed first and valued at six hundred rubles. It was carefully stored in the Tsar's Armory in a protective case made of red cloth.[30] During the war with Poland (1654–1656) and subsequently the war with Sweden, it formed part of Tsar Alexei Mikhailovich's campaign treasury.

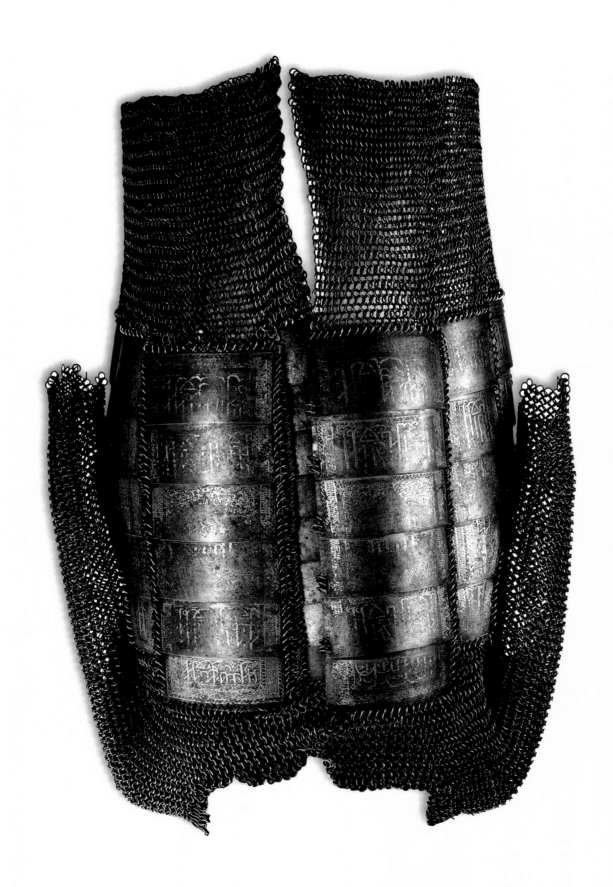

21. HELMET

Turkey, late 16th–early 17th century
Watered steel, silver, silk fabric

Known as a "Jericho cap," this ceremonial helmet is forged from watered steel. The entire surface of the helmet is chased with long grooves. Three gilded hinges attach the neck guard to the bowl. An adjustable nose guard with an openwork design is joined to the brim. Inside, the helmet still retains a soft lining of red patterned silk and ties of red and yellow satin. Almost the entire surface of the helmet is covered with a "lace" of inlaid gold and the following inscriptions from the Koran.

On the lower edge of the bowl: "Gladden the true believers with the promise of God's help and swift victory."

On the top of the bowl: "In the name of a good and merci-ful God."

On the bowl: "Eden is the living and eternal and inexhaust-ible God, and his essence is everywhere, on earth as in heaven, and without his will there can be no salvation for man. He knows all that men do and what has already been done by them; men know only what he has seen fit to reveal to them; his kingdom embraces heaven and earth and he creates it without effort, because he is all-powerful and glorious."

At the top and on the hinged cheek guards: "Oh God indivis-ible, immortal, most wise, righteous, holy."

On the neck guard: "I have sent you to enlighten the human race, while the sinners, having heard that you preach the teachings of the Al'Koran, will wish to confuse you with their gazes and, envying you, will begin to say, 'He is possessed by a devil.'"

On the top of the sliding nose guard: "There is no God but Allah, and Muhammad is his prophet."

Judging by documentary evidence, Afanasei Pronchishchev brought the helmet from Tsargrad (Istanbul) in 1633.[31] A particularly costly and important object, it is listed first in the 1687 inventory of the Great State Treasury, and it is also among the list of items that Tsar Alexei Mikhailovich took on his military campaigns of 1654–1656. The documents do not mention whether this helmet was a gift from the Turkish sultan Murad IV or whether Pronchishchev presented it to Tsar Mikhail Fedorovich on his own behalf.

In the summer of 1632 an embassy from the Russian tsar, with the nobleman Pronchishchev at its head, was dispatched from Moscow to Istanbul, where it was received with great honor. After reaching an accord with Sultan Murad IV, the embassy embarked on its return journey. Even though the ship was beset by a storm and the ambassadors were almost killed by the inhabitants of Kafa on the Crimean coast, Pronchishchev protected the valuables with which he had been entrusted and safely delivered them to the tsar. Among them was this highly prized helmet, with its elegant shape and exceptional ornamentation.

22. CAPARISON

Russia, Kremlin workshops, 17th century;
gilded satin: Turkey, mid-16th century
Gilded satin, satin, taffeta

Made of patterned gilded satin, this circular caparison is woven in bright green, scarlet, and yellow silk and gold threads on a white ground. Vertical parallel bands of curved stems bear large tulips worked in a fine design of narrow wavy leaves and small carnations and tulips. The weave rapport is fragmentary. The large pattern and white ground date the gold satin to the mid-sixteenth century and the reigns of both Sultan Süleyman the Magnificent in Turkey and Ivan the Terrible in Russia.

This is a "second cut" piece, which means it was sewn from other items and still retains the details and seam lines of those original garments. Several unevenly shaped pieces, such as sleeves with semicircular armholes and narrow straight hems, clearly betray their origins as parts of secular clothing. They could well be pieces from one of Tsar Ivan the Terrible's numerous robes. In addition to

describing several types of his clothing, the 1582 inventory of Tsar Ivan Vasilevich's domestic wardrobe notes that the fabrics used for many of his robes were acquired from Mustafa Çelebi, a Turkish merchant. Çelebi traveled twice to Russia, and on his first visit he brought a letter from Sultan Süleyman to the tsar. Entire garments, such as kaftans, state robes, and *chiugi* (narrow kaftans with elbow-length sleeves), that Çelebi presented are also listed in the inventory. In the sixteenth century the cut and basic features of the tsar's floor-length outer robes were similar to a Turkish kaftan, having either a freely flowing or a slightly fitted silhouette. Durable fabrics that would not crease or break into myriad folds when worn were ideally suited to this purpose. This type of fabric, called a "double-sided gilded satin" in Russian terminology, was also used for this horse caparison.

23. DAGGER AND SHEATH

Turkey, second half 16th century; blade: Iran, 16th century;
master: Mahmud, son of Mas'ud
Steel, nephrite, gold, diamonds, rubies

While the construction of the dagger is rather simple and archaic, the decorative use of precious stones, gold, and other rare materials, combined with its technique, distinguish it from traditional weapons. The double-edged steel blade is decorated on both sides with verses damascened in gold. The front of the blade is inscribed:

"A dream of your dagger wells up in [my] eye, like tears
Like the moon that swirls in the water hither and thither!"
"The willow draws the dagger into its shadow.
It seems to me that, even without a hand, it draws the dagger."
"May all your affairs go as you would like them,
May the ruler of the world be your protector."
On the back of the blade:

"Take the dagger and extract the heart from my breast, so that you might see our heart among the beloved."

"Each time your dagger spoke of vengeance, it brought the age into disorder with its bloodletting! With the refinement and purity of the stones that adorn it, it recalled a willow leaf covered with dew!"

"May you have peace [according to] your desire and may heaven be your friend,

May the creator of the world be your protector."

Also inscribed on the front is "O prophet and most renowned [people] of his line" and the name of the maker: "made by Mahmud son of Mas'ud." Unfortunately, nothing is known about this Iranian armorer. Only this dagger bears witness to his exceptional skill.

The hilt of the blade is damascened in gold on both sides with a stylized *chi* design. Carved of nephrite, the hilt and outer sheath are decorated with rows of table-cut rubies set in relief-encrusted gold mounts in the form of six-petaled rosettes. Slender, waving stems with miniature leaves are worked in the same technique but are flush with the surface. On the underside of the sheath a stylized design known as *rumi* is carried out in gold encrustation.[32] A gold crosspiece with the ends curled under form the dagger guard. Its outer side is decorated with precious stones, while the underside displays a large, brightly colored floral design in blue, green, and yellow enamel.

The dagger is first mentioned in the inventory of the Imperial Collection of Weapons of the St. Petersburg Rustkammer in 1810, but its origins might well be much earlier. The distinctive handling of the nephrite, encrusted with gold and set with precious stones, suggests it was made in the Ottoman Empire some time in the second half of the sixteenth century.[33] The blade was forged and decorated at the same time, probably in Iran. Enhanced with precious stones and colored enamel, the guard of the hilt was most likely made somewhat later, in the seventeenth century.

A dagger of similar construction, materials, and decorative style from the Rustkammer of the Emperors of the Holy Roman Empire in the Kunsthistorisches Museum in Vienna was included in the exhibition *The Age of Sultan Süleyman the Magnificent* at the National Gallery of Art in Washington, D.C., in 1987. The identical construction and decoration of the handle and sheath of both daggers provide a strong basis for suggesting they came from the same workshop or center of production. It is noteworthy that the construction and decoration of this blade mirror that of the dagger from Vienna, which was attributed to Ottoman workmen of the sixteenth century. A dagger with similar verses and an Iranian doubled-edged blade is in the State Hermitage (GE, inv. no. OR-504).[34]

24. SABER AND SHEATH FROM THE GRAND ATTIRE

Turkey, before 1656
Watered steel, wood, gold, emeralds, rubies,
sapphires, nephrite

This is one of the most richly adorned sabers of its type from the arsenal of the Russian autocrats in the seventeenth century. Its designation as a saber of the Grand Attire signifies it was part of the main set of ceremonial armor that the tsar used during military processions and inspections. The notation "Turkish forging" in the 1686/1687 inventory of the Armory indicates its Ottoman origins, as does the traditionally luxurious decoration of its handle and sheath. The masterful execution, the variety and complexity of techniques, and the rich materials all suggest it was created by jewelers in the workshops associated with the Ottoman imperial court.

Forged of watered steel and wedge shaped in section, the blade has medium curvature and a traditional double edge towards the point (*elman*). Unfortunately, the blade was polished, probably in the nineteenth century, which abraded the metal's distinctive pattern and texture. Incised in gold in an ornamental medallion on the upper part of the blade is the partially preserved Arabic inscription "May you pass your time in bliss."

A stylized design of rubies and emeralds set in encrusted gold mounts in the form six-petaled rosettes and with scrolls of tiny leaves decorates the saber's nephrite hilt. Soldered on both sides of the hilt's straight crosspiece are rubies and emeralds in large rectangular mounts.

Covered with fine gold leaf, the outer sheath of the saber is decorated with a carved stylized plant design, gems, and nephrite plaques encrusted with rubies in gold petal-shaped casts. Ornamenting the reverse side is a finely engraved stylized plant motif of shoots, rosettes, and buds on a flat-chased ground. A broad niello ribbon and niello-ornamented medallions also run the length of the scabbard. Complex designs of interwoven shoots are incised on the edge and in the medallions, creating a rich combination of dense black and bright gold. According to archival documents, a sumptuous belt made of lazurite silk braid with a gold mount adorned with diamonds once accompanied the saber.

This saber received extremely high status in the Tsar's Armory and was numbered first among the sabers of the Grand Attire in the 1686/1687 inventory of the Armory. "Aniska Almaznikov and others," appraisers at the Silver Row, valued it at 1,670 rubles. According to an inventory entry, Ivan Bulgakov, a member of the Merchants' Hundred (*gostinnaia sotnia*), presented the saber to the tsar on 10 December 1656. That date coincides with Greek merchants' importation of precious wares intended for Tsar Alexei Mikhailovich.

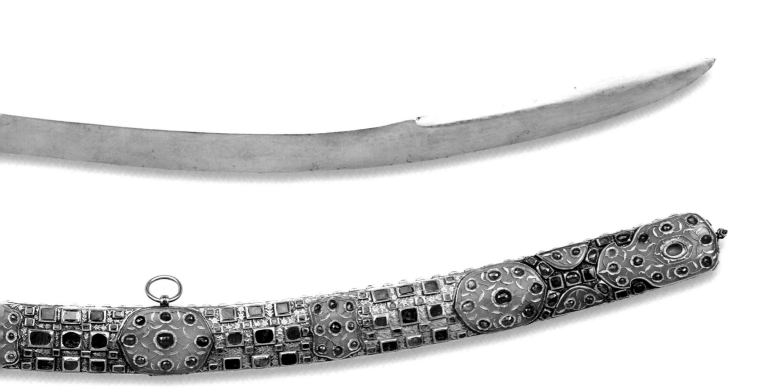

Gift of Tsarevich Seid-Burkhan Arsalanovich to Tsar Alexei Mikhailovich in 1653
Turkey, first half 17th century
Leather, silver cannetille, nephrite, rubies, emeralds,
glass, gold, silver, rock crystal

In archival documents of the Russian court, this flask is described as a *suleia.* (Its original name, transliterated from Arabic, was *matara.*) Such vessels were generally used to hold liquids, with the waterproof leather body keeping the contents cold. A stopper was attached to the body by a chain.

This leather *suleia* has the traditional trapezoidal form associated with drinking flasks that were attached to a rider's saddle or hung over a foot traveler's shoulder. Over time, such utilitarian objects often were transformed into status symbols for their well-to-do owners. The flask's shape resembles leather drinking vessels that have been excavated in burial sites in Central Asia and date as early as the fifth century BCE.

In addition to decorations made of silver cannetille, the vessel's surface, including the base, is embellished with oval and rectangular nephrite plaques. Others take the shape of stylized pomegranate fruit or gold rosette-shaped plaques. All are encrusted with gems in rosette mounts and plant motifs worked in gold wire. The stopper, made of rock crystal encrusted with gems, fits tightly in the neck, which is lined with a silver tube. A long fine twisted cord of silver cannetille and silk with a tassel on the end joins the stopper to the body.

The gold spout vaguely resembles a dragon's neck. It also has a stopper on a chain and is decorated with niello scales and a stylized plant design executed in carved relief. Niello on gold was one of the most widespread techniques used for Ottoman wares in the sixteenth and seventeenth centuries (cat. 24, 37). In the collection of the Kremlin Museums is another flask of somewhat different construction (inv. no. DK-463).

Rudolph II, the emperor of the Holy Roman Empire, received a sumptuously decorated leather flask from Sultan Murad III.[35] Artisans in the sultan's workshops used a variety of materials, including gold, to make such flasks. Gold water vessels held special significance in Ottoman court rituals. Manuscripts from the time of sultans Süleyman the Magnificent and Selim II describe the rulers being accompanied by courtiers who carry a sword — a symbol of the sultan's power — and a precious flask. From the reign of the Ottomans on, such flasks were associated with the sultan's supreme authority.

Inventories of the Tsar's Treasury indicate this *suleia* was a gift from Tsarevich Seid-Burkhan Arsalanovich to Tsar Alexei Mikhailovich on 2 August 1653.[36] Perhaps familiarity with the significance of the *matara* at the court of Istanbul influenced the tsarevich's choice of the gift.

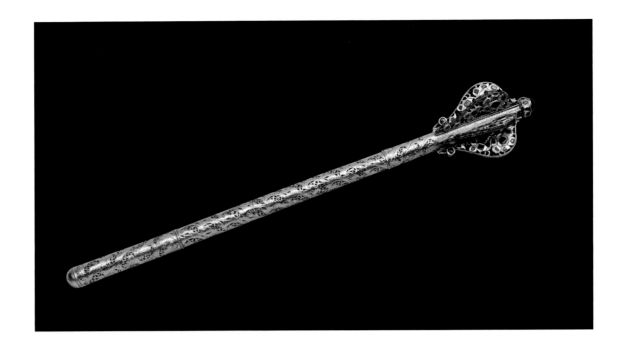

26. CEREMONIAL MACE

Turkey, Istanbul, mid-17th century
Gold, wood, garnets, emeralds, rubies, enamel

A *shestoper* (literally, six-flanged) was the name given in early Russia to weapons used against an opponent dressed in armor. The weapon's head consisted of six, usually steel, flanges. In addition to fighting maces, which formed part of a rider's weaponry in Europe and Asia as early as the sixteenth and seventeenth centuries, ceremonial maces such as this costly example symbolized military authority. On 1 June 1656 it was presented to Tsar Alexei Mikhailovich, together with other richly decorated weapons, articles of equipment, and horse trappings, by Dmitry Astafiev, a well-known merchant from Istanbul. It was called a *buzdygan* in the Inventory of Gifts of 1656. In both the Ottoman Empire and Russia, this was the same name given to staffs, maces, and other symbols of monarchical power that were presented to regional governors or military leaders when they assumed their posts. This mace was listed in the 1686/1687 inventory and ranked first in the section of *buzdygany*, its value set at 2,850 rubles.

Each of the six flanges is worked in a simple openwork design, with an outer ornamented gold rim. Soldered inside are costly plaques in the form of a rosette, a trefoil, and a tiny leaf with table-cut rubies and emeralds. Stems that link the plaques seem to glow with green and white enamel. The plaques' outer edges are embellished with a gold-colored design of slender stems with intertwining shoots set against a black enamel ground. A large garnet in a tall gold mount and framed with a band of emeralds crowns the top. The wooden handle, covered in gold, has an incised openwork design that spirals upwards from the lower part of the handle to combine harmoniously with the openwork plaques on the head. As a result, the mace possesses a magnificence that makes it a true masterpiece of Ottoman jewelry and armorial art in the mid-seventeenth century.

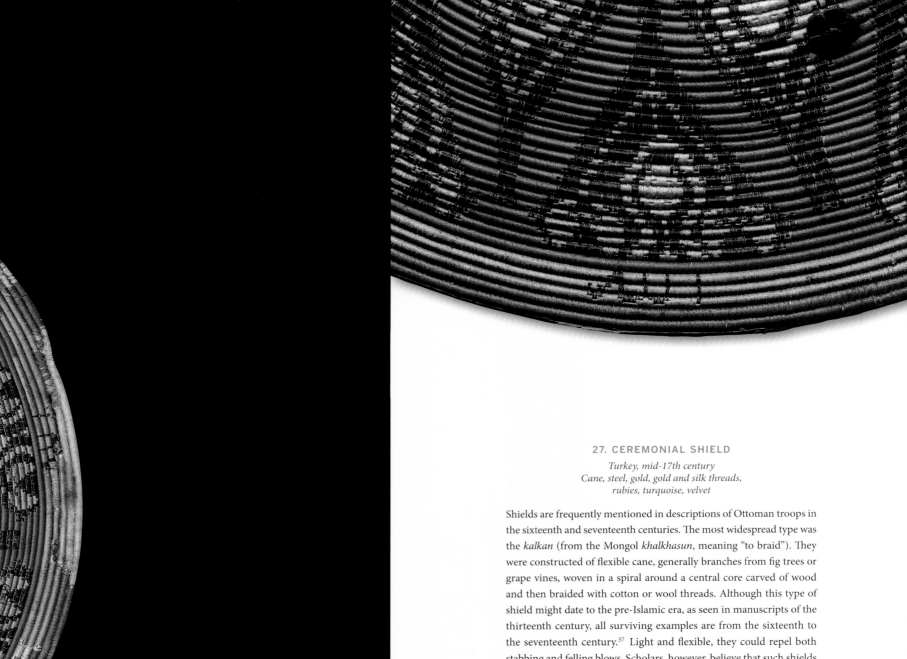

27. CEREMONIAL SHIELD

Turkey, mid-17th century
Cane, steel, gold, gold and silk threads,
rubies, turquoise, velvet

Shields are frequently mentioned in descriptions of Ottoman troops in the sixteenth and seventeenth centuries. The most widespread type was the *kalkan* (from the Mongol *khalkhasun*, meaning "to braid"). They were constructed of flexible cane, generally branches from fig trees or grape vines, woven in a spiral around a central core carved of wood and then braided with cotton or wool threads. Although this type of shield might date to the pre-Islamic era, as seen in manuscripts of the thirteenth century, all surviving examples are from the sixteenth to the seventeenth century.[37] Light and flexible, they could repel both stabbing and felling blows. Scholars, however, believe that such shields were largely used as ceremonial armor by this time.

This shield is decorated with a braid of silk thread, which creates an elegant and colorful pattern of large "lanceolate" medallions on the outer side. Embroidered several times around the edge is the Arabic inscription "Allah." Attached in the center front is a protruding gold knob (*umbon*) decorated in repoussé with twined bands and an incised gold design on a black ground. Turquoises and rubies set in gold mounts embellish the curving bands. A cord for hanging the shield and a small cushion to absorb the impact of blows are attached to rings on the inner side by small metal figured plaques. This ceremonial shield was presented to Tsar Alexei Mikhailovich on 16 January 1659 by the nobleman Vusat Eorgiev, the priest Gavrila Ivanov, and the treasurer Petr Ivanov in the name of Alexander, the tsar of Imereti (today a province of Georgia). It was kept in the Tsar's Treasury until 1663, when it was transferred to the Armory. More than twenty years later it was listed eighth in the inventory for 1686/1687.

28. CURTAIN

Russia, 17th century; velvet, Turkey, first half 17th century
Raised-pile gilded velvet, gilded fringe

In the 1640 inventory of the Tsar's Treasury, this curtain is mentioned as having been purchased from Afanasy Dmitriev, a Greek who came to Moscow as part of a Turkish embassy in 1630. It is constructed of two lengths of gilded velvet with a pattern of large carnations surrounded by denticulate leaves with tulips at the tips.

The large pattern and rich color scheme of dark red and gold lend a ceremonial, somewhat official flavor to the curtain.

A noticeably dense weave is created where the velvet nap does not cover the entire surface but instead alternates with sections of pattern woven with gold threads to form a smooth ground. Not surprisingly, such heavily textured textiles were readily used in the tsar's living quarters as large curtains and to line the walls of state apartments.

Turkey, late 17th century
Brocade, fringe, dyed homespun

A black patterned brocade, the ground of which is woven entirely of silver thread, distinguishes this caparison. Patterns of gold thread and white, light green, and light scarlet silk emphasize its functional components. Where the saddle rests is outlined in black and decorated with bunches of feathery leaves and small stylized fruits. Below, in the center of the caparison, is a large keel-shaped half-palmette surrounded by curving scrolls with large stylized flowers, tulips, buds, and leaves.

A border patterned with serrated leaves, flowers, and fruits frames three sides and extends to the lower section. Two rows of braided spun gold and red silk fringe run along the edges on three sides.

The large dimensions of the caparison, the placement of the embroidered pattern, and the compositional isolation of the saddle area place it in the group of horse coverings called *namety*, specially cut caparisons that are thrown over a saddle or simply placed over the croup of an unsaddled horse.

30. SAADAK COVER

Russia, 17th century; center panel: Turkey, first half 17th century;
border: Iran, first half 17th century
Embossed gilded velvet, taffeta, fringe

A *saadak* (a case for bow and arrows) served as a military symbol of the Russian tsar until the end of the seventeenth century. He carried a *saadak* and its cover during his inspection of troops, one of the official ceremonies of the Russian state.

The cover listed in the Armory inventory of 1686/1687 was sewn from two pieces of textiles, with the center panel created from a Turkish cushion cover. Such items made of textile pieces were an important component of Ottoman weaving production for both the domestic and export markets in the sixteenth and seventeenth centuries. Made of embossed gilded velvet on a dark red ground, the central rectangle contains an oval medallion woven in gold threads with a velvet twelve-point star in the middle. Small velvet stars visually anchor the corner bosses, which are woven of gold with figured edges. The use of a compositionally complete motif for the central panel of the cover effectively differentiated the tsar's *saadak* during court ceremonies.

Gilded striped velvet imported from Iran forms the surrounding border. The varying widths and patterns of the stripes keep them from being too monotonous. Small flower heads are woven in the wide stripes, while the narrow ones display smaller versions of the same motif. Adding further liveliness to the rhythmic composition are the slight slant of the small leaves, the flowers themselves, and the alternating colors of blue, green, brown, yellow, and gray (see left). The velvet pile visibly rises above the smooth surface of the ground, which is woven with spun silver threads.

31. SADDLECLOTH

Turkey, 17th century
Velvet, silk, gold threads

As a kind of saddlecloth that covers the horse's croup, the *cheprak* extends backwards from beneath the saddle. This rectangular *cheprak* is embroidered with gold and silver. Narrow bands with alternating designs are embroidered on plain scarlet velvet. Some bands contain two rows of stylized pomegranate flowers on curved stems with small five-petaled flowers. Others have geometrical garlands of stylized cypress, denticulate leaves, and floral rosettes. In the center of the upper section, gold embroidery borders the opening for the tail strap, which fastened to the saddle with a leather loop and attached to the horse's tail. On three sides the *cheprak* is edged with gilded velvet with gold loops. A yellow silk fabric serves as the lining, and an extension of the same fabric is covered by the saddle.

An unusually large number of Turkish *chepraks* embroidered with gold and silver entered the Tsar's Treasury in the 1650s. In 1656 alone, for instance, around fifty of them, embroidered with gold and seed pearls, were brought to Moscow from Istanbul. Several have been preserved in the collection of the Armory (Kremlin Museums, inv. nos. TK-587, TK-594, TK-595). This *cheprak* is probably among the gifts that Ivan Nastasov, a Greek living in Istanbul, presented to Tsar Alexei Mikhailovich and Tsarevich Alexei Alexevich in 1658.

32. SADDLE

Turkey, mid-17th century
Gold, silver, gold thread, rubies, emeralds, pearls,
wood, leather, velvet, braid

With the classic shape characteristic of the best Turkish craftsman-ship in the mid-seventeenth century, this saddle has a high, narrow front pommel and a broad sloping cantle that are joined by the flowing line of the seat. Plain scarlet velvet upholstery is adorned with gold embroidery. An edging of gold braid and a border of serrated leaves emphasize the saddle's handsome contours, with oval flaps at the sides and *izvesti* (parts of saddle boards) pro-jecting from under the saddle at front and back. A large ogival medallion is contained within a stylized plant motif on the seat. Repeated three times on each wing is a design of three pinecones on widening denticulate trunks with needle-shaped branches. Fruits resembling pinecones are embroidered on both the *izvesti* and the seat.

The pommel and cantle are decorated with gold repoussé figured plaques with rubies and emeralds framed in seed pearls. This unusual decorative technique suggests the saddle may have come into the Stable Treasury as a gift from Greek merchants. The income book of the Stable Treasury records that on 2 August 1656 Avram Rodionov and Dmitry Konstantinov presented Tsar Alexei Mikhailovich and Tsarevich Alexei Alexevich with two Turkish sad-dles embroidered in gold and with distinctive gold plaques set with rubies and emeralds framed in pearls.[38] In the inventories of the Stable Treasury from the second half of the seventeenth century and the first third of the eighteenth, the saddle is listed as number fifteen in the "gold saddles" section and is described as a "Turkish saddle." Gilded bronze stirrups were attached in the seventeenth century.

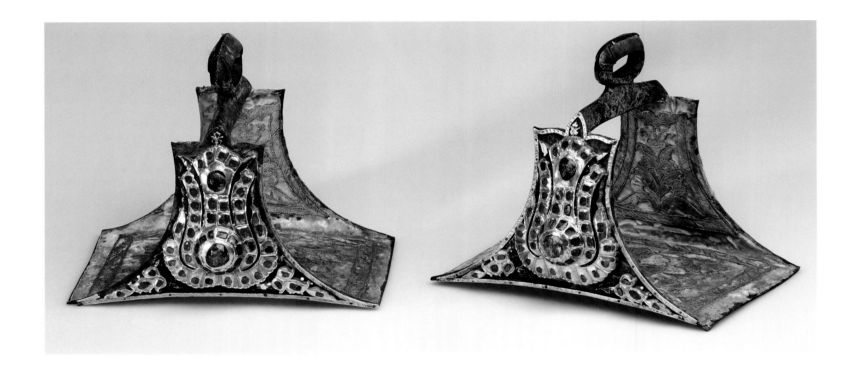

33. PAIR OF STIRRUPS

Turkey, mid-17th century
Gold, rubies, emeralds, iron, velvet, gold thread

Turkish stirrups of the seventeenth century are distinguished by their massiveness and rich decoration. They were often forged of silver or gold and adorned with gems. The Armory collection has preserved a large group of Turkish stirrups from this period. They all have straight, triangular sides that narrow towards the top, wide elongated bases, and rectangular loops for the stirrup leathers. These wide-based stirrups allow the rider to sit more securely on his mount. On the outside, gold plate is engraved with a design of pomegranate fruits covered in translucent emerald green enamel and decorated with large rubies and emeralds. Light-colored velvet embroidered with silver wire lines the inner surfaces.

With their characteristic shape and fine craftsmanship, these elegant stirrups may have been produced in the workshops serving the Ottoman court. Horse trappings of this high degree of luxury and meticulous workmanship entered the Stable Treasury of Tsar Alexei Mikhailovich in the mid-seventeenth century as part of diplomatic gifts and trade imports from Turkey. In the 1706 inventory of the Stable Treasury the stirrups are listed as belonging to a saddle of Russian workmanship that was recorded as number ninety-eight.[39] In this instance the assigned number does not reflect the saddle's actual status in the Tsar's Treasury. By the end of the seventeenth century the Stable Treasury contained two hundred saddles of various kinds, each listed under a general number. Since these "Turkish stirrups with gems . . . large gold plaques in which faceted emeralds are studded" were added to a new *archak* (saddle) in the 1680s, they clearly were the finest in the Tsar's Treasury.

34. PAIR OF STIRRUPS

Turkey, mid-17th century
Iron, gold, pearls, rubies, emeralds, fabric, gold thread

A unique feature of the decoration of these forged and gilded iron stirrups is that they are enhanced with fabric both inside and out, and the sides are entirely covered in seed pearls. Gold plaques in the form of cypresses with emeralds and rubies are arranged on the pearl ground. These are surrounded by four small gold plaques shaped like denticulate leaves with the same gems. A narrow border of gold braid marks the edge. Red and gold silk lines each stirrup. Embroidered in the center of the base, under the rider's foot, is an eight-petaled flower with radiating serrated leaves and four small six-petaled rosettes.

Stirrups that Turkish merchants presented to Tsar Alexei Mikhailovich in the mid-seventeenth century have a similar decoration. Gold plaques with emeralds and rubies framed in pearls likewise adorn saddlecloths (Kremlin Museums, inv. nos. TK-594, TK-595) and saddles (Kremlin Museums, inv. nos. K-233, K-228) made of silver brocade (*altabas*). The pearl stirrups, however, are absolutely unique and are without equal in museum collections around the world.

According to inventories of the Stable Treasury from 1687 to 1711, these Ottoman stirrups were attached to a cushioned saddle of Russian workmanship. That particular *archak* in a silver and niello mount was covered with light green velvet and embroidered with gold wire. This further confirms that in ceremonial processions of the time, no clear distinction was made between horse trappings of Russian, Turkish, Polish, or German manufacture. Saddles, stirrups, harnesses, caparisons, and other adornments were used together, regardless of whether they were made in Moscow or Istanbul. This lent the horse's trappings a special sense of luxury and beauty.

These stirrups were utilized in royal processions on several occasions. By the end of the seventeenth century some of the stones and pearls had fallen off, and the fabric lining had become worn and darkened. The last time they were temporarily removed from the Stable Treasury was in 1728, when they were used during the ceremonial entry into Moscow of Emperor Peter II at the time of his coronation.

35, 36. BRIDLE AND CHEST STRAPS

Turkey, before 1622/1623
Gold, silver, rubies, pearls, turquoise,
nephrite, leather, braid

Silver gilt plates with a chased design entirely cover the bridle and chest straps made of leather and braid of multicolored silk and gold threads. Narrow rectangular plaques set with three turquoises in tall mounts alternate with wide ones that have four turquoises at the corners. Gold encrustation and three rubies complement the oval nephrite insets in the center. Plaques with nephrite insets alternate with others that have apertures filled with round seed pearls and surround a turquoise set in a gold mount.

Large round plates that mark where the head and forehead straps join are meticulous examples of the Ottoman jeweler's art (see right). Their edges are chased and adorned with large turquoises in high mounts. The central part, filled with insets of dark nephrite with a figured edge, is furthered ornamented with an unusually dense and carefully worked pattern of gold encrustation that takes the form of small leaves and flower petals set with rubies and turquoises.

Jewelers in Istanbul often combined gold encrustation with precious stones in items made of nephrite and nephrite plaques (see cat. 23, 24, 25, 37, 38, 42). Decorating precious metal with insets of seed pearls, however, is an extremely rare technique, one found only in the decoration of this bridle. The compilers of the Stable Treasury inventory called these insets "pearl circlets." One such pearl circlet is placed within a nephrite plate on the forehead section of the bridle to accommodate a round hole that was drilled there. Similar pearl circlets, though smaller and positioned on round nephrite plates, also appear on the central plate of the chest strap (see left). In addition, the central chest plate is adorned with four more almond-shaped nephrite plaques, each with a large convex nephrite insert in the center and a large turquoise in a tall mount on a chased ground.

In the 1706 inventory of the Stable Treasury the set of bridle and chest straps is listed as number fifteen with the notation, "Taken from the Foreign Office in 131 [1622/1623] price 157 rubles."[40] The high value assigned to these items at the time they entered the Treasury is based on both the precious materials used and the exceptional level of artistic execution. Judging by the date of their transfer from the Foreign Treasury, they were in all probability gifts to Tsar Mikhail Fedorovich brought by the Great Embassy of Sultan Osman II in 1621. Unfortunately, no further documentation about this gift has been found.

Thomas Cantacuzene, scion of a noble Greek family, headed this diplomatic mission of 1621, just as he did those of 1627, 1630, and 1633. One of the two bridles with rubies and diamonds that Cantacuzene presented to Tsar Mikhail Fedorovich in 1633 is preserved in the Armory collection (Kremlin Museums, inv. no. K-222).

37, 38. BRIDLE AND CHEST STRAPS

Turkey, 17th century
Leather, silver, rubies, emeralds, turquoise,
nephrite, silk, braid

This set of bridle and chest straps is decorated in a unified style. Wide straps of soft leather are sewn with braids of colored silk and gold and are strung with silver-gilt openwork plaques with a niello plant design (see next page). Pieces of red, yellow, and blue silk inserted beneath the openwork plates give the set a distinctive elegance. The massive central forehead plate is treated differently (see top right). Its surface is enhanced with a niello pattern, large stones set in tall mounts, and rhomboid insets of nephrite encrusted with rubies and emeralds. Gold petals and leaves frame the gems. The same decoration, typical of Ottoman art, was also used on other square and round nephrite insets where the bridle and chest straps join.

The set entered the Kremlin Treasury in 1655, after the death of boyar Nikita Ivanovich Romanov, a kinsman of the tsar who died without heirs. It was listed first in an inventory of Romanov's "horse attire," which numbers some two hundred items. This set begins the section of silver harness with gems in the 1706 inventory. Since the bridle initially had an iron mouthpiece and reins of silk braid with silver buckles, the set at one time was listed among harnesses with iron mouthpieces. A bridle and chest straps created in a similar technique, dated 1626, are found in the collection of the Royal Swedish Armory.[41]

87

39, 40, 41. BRIDLE, CHEST STRAPS, AND CRUPPER

Presented by Ambassador Rusan Beg to Tsar Mikhail Fedorovich in 1624/1625
Turkey, before 1625; Braid, leather, gold, silver, rubies, turquoises, peridots

These straps for the head, chest, and croup of a horse are similarly decorated, with the leather straps sewn with gold braid in a geometric pattern. The braid is threaded with figured plaques embellished with large, faceted peridots — semiprecious stones of a grass green color — set in a delicate plant design enlivened with niello. The gold points on the strap ends are decorated in the same way. Particularly notable is the central plaque that joins the chest straps (see right). Octagonal in shape, it has a raised center and a peridot in the middle, the alternate facets of which are worked in niello with a chased plant design. Gold plaques mark the intersections of the head and forehead straps, and the tips are ornamented with rubies and turquoises.

Of the numerous costly sets of trappings in the Tsar's Treasury, this gold harness was given a particularly high value. It is listed first in all inventories of the Stable Treasury, and Russian sovereigns used it throughout the seventeenth century. Before 1687 the set was restored in the Kremlin workshops: the iron bit was replaced by a massive mouthpiece that allowed the rider to control the horse at a slow and solemn gait suitable for ceremonial processions. This bit replacement required changes in the construction and joins of the bridle straps. The original gold and niello buckles might have been supplemented with new clasps of silver and gilt ornamented with

carving and chasing. The braid on the tail straps was lengthened by attaching narrow gold braid of a different geometric pattern to the ends of the straps (see top left). Added to the bridle's muzzle strap and the tailpiece are carved gilded plates with openings for securing the large round tassels of twisted silk that were mandatory for parade trappings. The remaining tassel on the tailpiece (on the horse's croup) was made from dark red silk with a woven knob in the center.

Information on when and from where the set entered the Tsar's Treasury comes from the 1706 inventory of the Stable Treasury. According to records, Ambassador Rusan Beg presented it as a gift from the shah of Iran to Tsar Mikhail Fedorovich in 133 (1624/1625). The costly set was taken to the State Treasury and valued at three hundred rubles. Archival documents in the Foreign Treasury confirm these facts. In the Acts of the Persian Court for 1618–1624 it is mentioned that Rusan Beg, the ambassador to the Iranian shah, brought to Tsar Mikhail Fedorovich "as gifts" a saddle and bridle trimmed with gold and precious stones, "sent to the Shah by the Turkish tsar." In other words, the gold harness taken to the Moscow Kremlin as a diplomatic gift from Iran was actually made in the palace workshops of Istanbul. This underscores the high regard with which Ottoman craftsmen and their artistic traditions were held in Iran.

42. BOWL

Gift from Georgios Panagiotis
to Tsar Mikhail Fedorovich in 1632
Turkey, first third 17th century
Nephrite, gold, emeralds, rubies, sapphires

Flat and relief encrustation decorate the body of this nephrite bowl. Gold wires delineate four stylized medallions that contain table-cut rubies, emeralds, and sapphires on multicolored foil and in raised rosette-shaped mounts. The jewels are aligned to form discernible crosses. Such Christian motifs are not unusual in Ottoman and Safavid art of the sixteenth and seventeenth centuries. This selection of precious stones, however, is uncommon in that sapphires were rarely used in decorating ceremonial vessels. Combinations of rubies and emeralds were more typical, especially in the seventeenth century, when they were often paired with diamonds or rock crystal (cat. 23–26, 33, 34, 37, 38, 43–48, 64).

The crown and scalloped base of the bowl have a gold mount with figured medallions and floral designs favored in the art of this period. The decoration is executed in carved relief, a technique in which Ottoman jewelers were especially skilled.

Georgios Panagiotis, an Orthodox subject of the Ottoman Empire and scion of an illustrious family from the former Byzantine Empire, presented the bowl to Tsar Mikhail Fedorovich. Panagiotis visited Moscow with Ahmed Aga, the ambassador of Sultan Murad IV. While his nephew took part in the reception held in the tsar's palace, Panagiotis himself was not present at the audience. Even so, his gifts to the tsar and the patriarch, like those that Archimandrite Amphilochios offered from Patriarch Cyril I Lukaris, are mentioned in the documents of the Treasury as having been presented on 20 February 1632 in the Faceted Chamber. In addition to the bowl, the tsar received a red velvet carpet, and the patriarch was given a valuable set of liturgical vessels and covers. Patriarch Filaret's gifts were valued at twice those presented to the tsar. Such precious vessels were usually kept in the Workshop Chamber of the Kremlin or in the apartments of the tsar's palace.

43. TANKARD

Gift from Patriarch Cyril I Lukaris to Tsar Mikhail Fedorovich in 1632
Turkey, first third 17th century
Rock crystal, gold, rubies, emeralds

Pomegranate flowers on long curved stems with leaves — one of the most widely used decorative motifs in Ottoman art — enliven the tall, cylindrical rock-crystal body of this tankard. Some of the flowers are made of table-faceted precious stones in rosette mounts, and others are suggested by fine gold threads. Two kinds of gold encrustation (either flush with the surface or in relief) on semiprecious stone and porcelain were known in the history of Ottoman jewelry during this period. This tankard features both types. The gold wire that forms the design of stems and shoots is flush with the surface of the crystal body, while the rubies and emeralds in the rosette mounts are in relief. Stylized tulips with curved stems and rosette mounts, in addition to the many-petaled rosettes, are used for the relief encrustation. A favorite flower in the gardens of the Ottoman sultans, tulips were frequently depicted on textiles, ceramics, tiles, and miniatures as early as the sixteenth century.

The gold base with its serrated edge is decorated with leaf-shaped cartouches filled with a small "carpet" plant design, executed in carved relief. This form of carving was widely used by Turkish goldsmiths in the sixteenth and seventeenth centuries. Quite likely the body of the tankard was made at an earlier date. The crystal handle is of a different quality and may have been added to the smooth cylindrical glass at the same time as the encrustation and the now-missing lid.

Patriarch Cyril I Lukaris sent the tankard as a gift to Tsar Mikhail Fedorovich. Archimandrite Amphilochios, the patriarch of Constantinople, and many other religious and secular figures visited Moscow with the embassy of Ahmed Aga, the official representative of Sultan Murad IV. Only a few secular Orthodox subjects of the sultan attended the audience in the Faceted Chamber on 20 February 1632, and Patriarch Cyril's gifts to the tsar, the tsarevich, and the patriarch went directly to the storerooms. The gifts sent to the tsar were the most costly; the tankard was valued at 150 rubles. The tsar's return gift of sables, sent as a mark of gratitude, was valued at twice that amount.

Documents record one more occasion on which a crystal wine bowl in a gold mount was given to Tsar Mikhail Fedorovich. It came from Ambassador Thomas Cantacuzene in 1630, but it did not enter the Tsar's Treasury. It may have remained in the personal apartments of the tsar without being appraised.

44. BOWL

Turkey, Istanbul, 17th century
Agate, gold, rubies, emeralds, rock crystal

An inlay of gold wire delineates the ogival figured medallions that decorate this small bowl. Scattered over the oval medallions are elongated leaves on curved intersecting stems that end in gold rosettes containing table-cut emeralds and rose- and table-cut rubies. In the center of each medallion is rose-cut rock crystal set over light blue foil. A stylized plant design enlivened with emeralds links the three medallions. Each of the precious stones is mounted in a gold rosette with engraved rays, as was typical of seventeenth-century Ottoman design. The manner of decorating the gold mounts, the composition, and the encrustation technique are all typical of Turkish art of this period. Using rock crystal to simulate diamonds, however, is a rare and original technique of Turkish jewelers. The combination of colored and transparent precious stones on this bowl suggests it dates to the second half of the seventeenth century. Originally the base of the bowl may have had a gold foot, and there might have been a lid. Items of this shape were themselves often used as lids for other vessels.

At an earlier period, for example, in 1630, wine goblets made of sardonyx (a type of chalcedony) entered the Tsar's Treasury as gifts from Greek merchants who were members of diplomatic delegations. Two years later, in 1632, one member of an embassy, known in Russia as Onton Spetsiiar, brought to the court an "*aspidnaia* [amber or agate] bratina . . . mounted in gold with rubies and emeralds."

45, 46. DISHES FOR SCENT BOTTLES

Turkey, Istanbul, first half 17th century
Rock crystal, gold, rubies, emeralds, paper

Each of these dishes for scent bottles has a central inset of rock crystal and a carved gold mount edged with multicolored precious stones. A floral design, executed in carved relief, decorates the mount. Floral scrolls and intertwining stems, combined with grooves and arcs, are chased in relief. One particularity of the decoration is the use of different shaped settings for the table-cut rubies and emeralds, which are attached to metal mounts and the central transparent insets. Stones in petaled rosettes, typical of encrusted semiprecious stones and porcelain, are set in the rock crystal, while stones in closed settings enhance the gold mount.

Such items entered the Tsar's Treasury and the Patriarchal Sacristy, together with scent bottles, as part of sets presented by Turkish diplomats and merchants. Dishes that accompanied scent bottles were called "saucers" in the inventories of the Tsar's Treasury.

47. SCENT BOTTLE

Turkey, first half 17th century
Rock crystal, gold, rubies, emeralds

The faceted crystal body of the scent bottle is encrusted with scrolls and leaves, while the neck displays a net pattern of gold wire. The flush encrustation is combined with encrustation in relief. Table-cut rubies and emeralds with an underlay of foil are mounted in gold rosettes. An open-work carved design and a pattern of flowers characteristic of Ottoman art, executed in carved relief, decorate the gold mount.

Similar bottles were brought to Moscow on several occasions as gifts from sultans and members of the mercantile elite, predominantly Greeks. No specific mention of this bottle is found in the Kremlin's documents, which suggests it did not enter the Treasury but instead went straight to the tsar's private apartments. In 1656 Ivan Nastasov and Dmitry Konstantinov, two merchants well known in Moscow, visited the court of Tsar Alexei Mikhailovich accompanied by a group of petitioners. One member, Dementy Petrov, presented the tsar with a "crystal vessel with a lid, beneath it a dish with a crystal center in gold, with rubies and emeralds."

In the inventories of the Tsar's Treasury, bottles of this shape were often called pepper pots. In 1555 the Greek merchant Fedor Ivanov gave to Alexei Mikhailovich "a crystal vessel, like a pepper pot . . . mounted in gold with stones, rubies, and emeralds, a gold base without stones . . ." valued at seven hundred rubles.

Bottles much like this one and in the collections of the Kremlin Museums may have had similar "diplomatic biographies." Items made of semiprecious stones and amber, such as jewelry and watches, were generally kept in the Workshop Chamber, but occasionally they were transferred to the Tsar's Treasury. A major transfer of crystal items took place in January 1644. Mentioned on the list is a gold-mounted crystal pepper pot in a light blue velvet case.

99

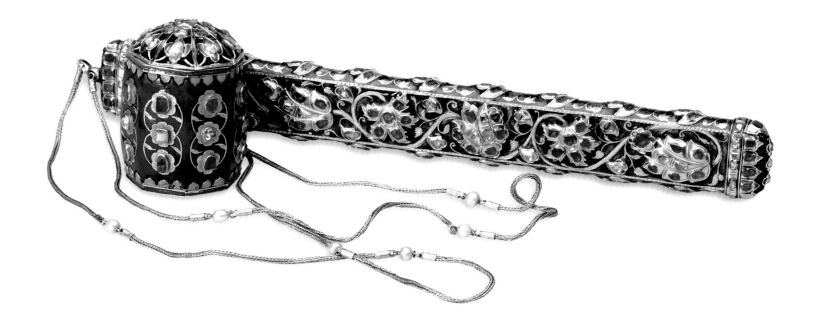

48. WRITING SET

Turkey, 1660s–1670s
Gold, silver, lazurite, diamonds, rubies, pearls

The writing set consists of a pencil box and an inkwell made of lazurite, a rare material in the decorative arts of Turkey. It is flat encrusted with scrolls and leaves of gold wire, as well as with precious stones set in gold petal-shaped rosettes worked in relief. The openwork lid is formed of flowers that resemble gold tulips set with rose-cut diamonds in the middle and joined by green enamel leaves. Encircling the base is a design of flowers, much like dog roses, applied in multicolored translucent enamel on an engraved surface. This technique, widely used in seventeenth-century Ottoman jewelry, must have been a source of pride for Istanbul craftsmen, particularly those associated with the imperial court. The engraved surface increased the area of the metal base that came into contact with the enamel, making it more durable and also giving the translucent enamel a special luster and glow.

Translucent green enamel applied over the engraving creates a ground for the decoration of the pencil box that is attached to the inkwell (see left). Designs of jewels enhance the box, with gold and ruby plaques in the form of large stylized carnations, fruits resembling pomegranates outlined with rubies and diamonds on curving stems, and tulips worked in light blue enamel. Similar carnations, pomegranates, and tulips frequently appear on fabrics, ceramics, tiles, and miniatures.[42] From the 1630s to the 1660s the combina-

tion of table-cut rubies and rose-cut diamonds, as seen here, was especially popular.

Costly inkwells, along with a variety of drinking vessels, flasks, serving dishes, scent bottles, and small caskets, formed the nucleus of the sultan's treasury.[43] Such items were often brought to the Muscovite court as gifts to the tsar and members of his family by leading representatives of Istanbul's Greek population and emissaries of the Orthodox church. They are listed among the gifts received from Turkish embassies in 1630 and 1631/1632. Ambassador Thomas Cantacuzene, for example, presented an inkwell to Tsarevich Alexei Mikihailovich in 1630. Later, as part of the embassy of 1631/1632, he offered Patriarch Filaret a nephrite inkwell in a gold mount decorated with rubies and emeralds.[44] A current assumption that this inkwell came to Moscow in connection with Cantacuzene's diplomatic mission of 1632 has yet to be verified through documentation. It is not mentioned in the list of gifts from that embassy.[45]

According to the inventory of Tsar Fedor Alexevich's personal effects, compiled after his death in 1682, this inkwell initially belonged to his elder brother, Tsarevich Alexei Alexevich, who died at an early age.[46] The older tsarevichs in the Romanov family often received gifts from foreign visitors, particularly those coming from the Ottoman Empire.

101

49. POCKET WATCH WITH CALENDAR

Mechanism and face: Geneva, mid-17th century; case: Istanbul, mid-17th century
Metal, gold, silver, diamonds, enamel

Two pocket watches with mechanisms from Geneva and cases made in Istanbul were formerly in the Tsar's Treasury and are now housed in the Armory. Both have a complex decorative design, but only this watch includes a calendar. Its massive oval body of cast gold is covered with translucent green enamel over an engraved surface, which makes the enamel appear to glow from within. Large table-cut and rose-cut diamonds with colored foil underneath them are mounted in settings of denticulate leaves, rosettes, tulips, and other stylized flowers. The interior of the lid is decorated with polychrome enamel: red, green, and dark blue dog roses and hyacinths on spiraling stems are scattered over a white opaque surface. Much like tulips, carnations, violets, and dog roses, irises grew in the gardens of the sultans and were often used to embellish Ottoman decorative art.[47]

Images of heroes from classical mythology are engraved on the dial face. Equipped with five hands, the face features dials for the hour, date, days of the week, months, and phases of the moon.

The mechanism has a balance spring with a catgut-wound fusee and a spindle escape wheel. Details of the mechanism are treated no less elegantly than the case. The drum, crown, and escape wheels are engraved with floral motifs, the trapezoidal bars that join the dial plate and the reverse plate are colored with enamel, and the escutcheon covering the balance is decorated with an openwork plant design. A screw attaches the escutcheon to a plate decorated with extremely fine floral motifs in niello. In addition to carved relief on gold, encrustation, and enamel on engraving, applying niello on gold and silver was a technique that Turkish jewelers used with great expertise throughout the seventeenth century (cat. 38).

Miniature watches with a complex mechanism and in a costly case were rarely included among the gifts that European diplomats and merchants from Turkey brought to Russia. Traditionally this watch is linked to the arrival in Moscow in 1658 of a representative of the Ottoman Empire's trading class, who was known in Russia by the name Ivan Anastasov (Nastasov).[48]

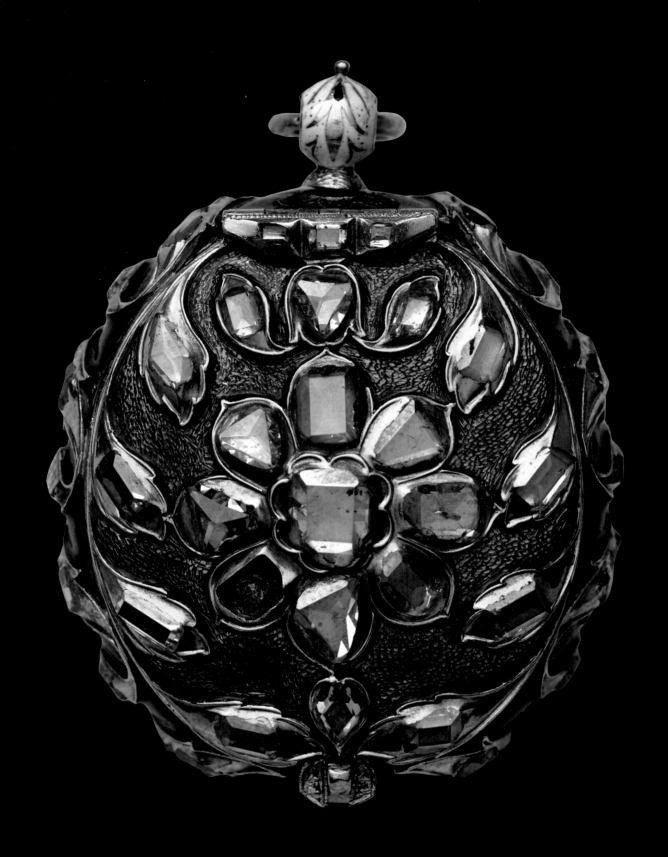

THE RUSSIAN RESPONSE

106

50, 51. CUFFS FOR A HORSE
Russia, Moscow Kremlin workshops, 17th century
Silver

Wide silver guards were a characteristic part of ceremonial Russian horse trappings in the seventeenth century. The horse's front legs were fitted with a pair of cuffs, and sometimes two pairs were fitted on both front and back legs.

In preparation for various ceremonial processions, the Kremlin workshops produced dozens and even hundreds of such decorative coverings for horses. This set was one of eleven pairs made in 1686/1687, and it was first mentioned in the 1687 inventory of the Stable Treasury.

Sparkling with gilding, these ornate coverings consist of two curved strips of silver joined by a hinge. The entire surface is chased with a plant design of curving stems and leaves that stand out distinctly from the indented ground. To protect the horse's legs, small slits for attaching soft protective pads of velvet, taffeta, or silk line each edge.

52. ORNAMENTAL HORSE CHAIN
Russia, Moscow Kremlin workshops, 17th century
Silver

Important elements of ceremonial trappings in seventeenth-century Russia were the massive silver chains that jingled with every movement of the horse. In the daily records of the tsar's court, special mention was made of these unusual adornments used during royal processions and receptions of foreign diplomats. For instance, on 16 April 1651 Tsar Alexei Mikhailovich set out for the court village of Pokrovskoe, and the forty horses led by court stablemen wore the Grand Attire with silver chains and neck tassels. More than eighty silver chains created in the Kremlin workshops are today in the Armory collection.

B. Tanner, a member of the Polish embassy of 1678, described the "magnificent" horse trappings of the ranks of the Stable Treasury. "Extending in a semicircle from either side of the bit to the front saddle pommel they wore silver and sometimes gold chains covered with various designs, three fingers thick, making the horses start at the jangling."[49] Despite the fact that most viewers could only see the procession from a distance, Kremlin craftsmen produced the clanging chains with great care and artistry (see right).

Although intended to be worn by the tsar's horse in ceremonial processions, this unusual adornment fulfilled a practical purpose. Its weight exceeds five kilograms, and its length is almost four meters. Each of the twenty-one links was forged from broad strips of silver, gilded and decorated with a meticulously worked chased design and bent into figure-eight shapes. Some links have geometric patterns, others a plant motif, and still others depict lions, unicorns, griffins, and fantastic birds among flowers. A cast double-headed eagle ends the chain.

53. TASSEL

Russia, Moscow Kremlin workshops, 17th century
Silver, braid, pearls, gold threads

Among the oldest items of horse decoration are neck tassels, which initially served as amulets and later signified horsemen who had reached manhood. They symbolized power and rank in Russia as early as the sixteenth century. On the Tsar Cannon in the Moscow Kremlin, cast by order of Tsar Fedor Ivanovich in 1586 in the Moscow cannon foundry, the Russian ruler is depicted astride a horse that wears a neck tassel. Four horse tassels are listed in the inventory of Boris Godunov's arsenal from the same period.[50] Most of the horse attire in the Saddle Treasuy of Tsar Vasily Shuisky (1610) included neck tassels (*nauz*) of silk and silver or "horsetail" tassles (*bobolev khvost*) made of horsehair.[51] Throughout the seventeenth century neck tassels were an essential part of the Grand Attire, and specific craftsmen at the Stable Treasury specialized in their production.

Dates can be assigned to six of the twenty neck tassels listed in the inventory of the Stable Treasury (1687–1706). The earliest "horsetails" in the Armory collection date to 1615–1617 and the earliest tassels to 1621–1622. This tassel, first mentioned in the inventory of 1687 to 1706, is listed twelfth without any indication of the year it entered the Treasury: "A chased silver gilt *nauz* (round top) with lions and unicorns . . . value 7 rubles."[52]

Made of three silver cords, the long tassel consists of four shorter silver tassels separated by small globes of seed pearls. The orb-shaped tip is chased with mythological and heraldic images. In the upper part are seen a winged unicorn, a lion, a winged *polkan* (the Russian version of a mythological centaur), and a depiction of the capture of Samson, dressed in armor, with a lion and birds. Eight chased openwork rosette-stars occupy the lower section. A braid of red silk attached the silver loop of the tassel to the bridle and suspended it from the horse's neck.

54. PAIR OF STIRRUPS

Russia, Moscow Kremlin workshops, 17th century
Silver, iron, braid

Mounted in silver, these stirrups were attached by straps to a saddle edged with bright silk braid. Both the saddle and stirrups, made by Kremlin masters in the seventeenth century, form a single set that was recorded under the same number in Treasury inventories.

The yoke-shaped stirrups with oval bases are forged of iron, but a finely gilded silver frame completely covers the black metal.

A carved plant design decorates the smooth silver surface of the hoops and the edge of the base. To underscore that the stirrups as well as the saddle belonged to the Russian tsar, the carved images of double-headed eagles with crowns placed in rosette-shaped cartouches are found on the base of the stirrups, beneath the rider's heels.

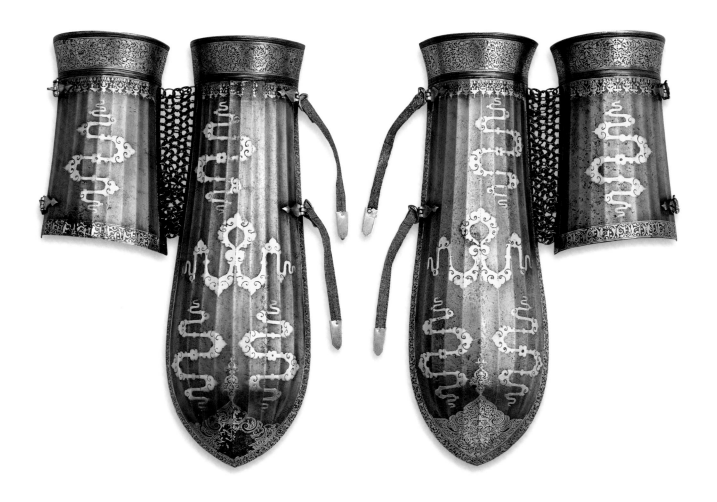

57. PAIR OF ARMGUARDS
Russia, Moscow Armory, first half 17th century; master: Nikita Davydov
Watered steel, braid

Armguards formed part of the armor that protected the outside of the forearm and the inner wrist. Made of forged steel, the elbows are shaped like an arrow and the wrist pieces are curved outwards. They are decorated with fluted gooves that have a gilded swirling design, a border inlaid in gold around the edge, and a small gold design on the elbows and wrists. Each armguard has two gilded buckles and two buckle plates, each with a small strap. The wrist guards (*cherevtsy*) are intact, joined to the armguards with five rows of armor-clad rings.

These armguards "of red iron made by Nikita Davydov" are listed third in the Armory inventory of 1686/1687 and valued at one hundred rubles. Its text suggests that in the 1680s they were

repaired and reinforced, perhaps with braid laces, buckles, and belt loops. Nikita Davydov made the armguards in the Turkish manner and evidently followed a specific model. A pair of armguards of Turkish workmanship with an almost identical decorative schema is preserved in the Armory (Kremlin Museums, inv. no. OR-4063). This second pair entered the Tsar's Treasury in 1630 and is listed second in the inventory of 1686/1687. Like the pair made by Davydov, it is valued at one hundred rubles.

Nikita Davydov, a first-class master, worked in the Armory from approximately 1613 to 1664. As an "armorer and gunsmith," he created magnificent helmets, harquebuses, pistols, and armor intended for the express use of the tsars.

58, 59. PAIR OF AMBASSADORIAL AXES

Turkey, early 17th century
Steel, gold, silver, wood

At the court of the Russian tsars in the sixteenth and seventeenth centuries ambassadorial axes served as ceremonial weapons carried by the tsar's bodyguards during solemn receptions of foreign ambassadors — hence their name. Their origins and symbolic meaning are not entirely clear, and no direct comparisons are known. Just eight such axes, of both Russian and Ottoman origin, are mentioned in the inventories of the Armory from 1647 and 1686/1687. This particular pair, called "Turkish," is listed first in deference to their great antiquity. Attributions in seventeenth-century inventories are based both on the steel heads of the axes with their rounded blades and on the ornamental strips inscribed in gold around the blade edges and with a darker shade of gold on the butt. The double-headed eagles damascened in a lighter gold were evidently added by Kremlin masters. In all likelihood the axe handles, edged with chased silver, were also produced later by Russian masters in the Kremlin workshops.

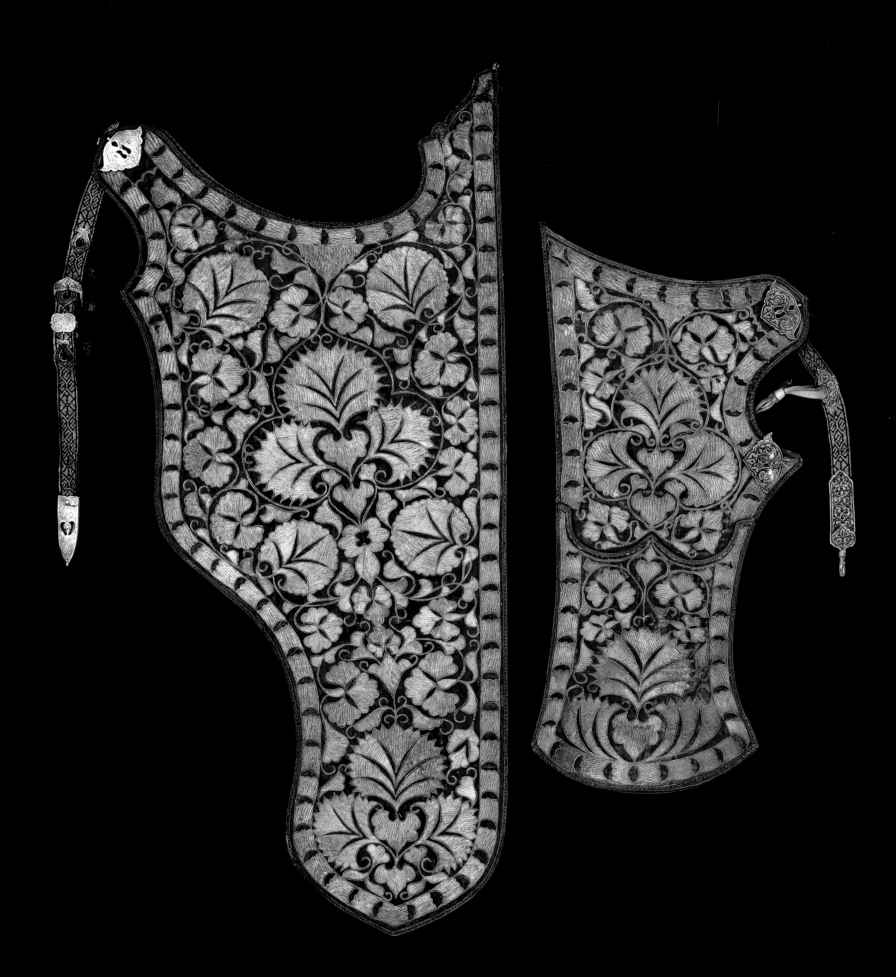

60. QUIVER AND BOW CASE

Russia, Moscow, 17th century
Leather, velvet, silver, silver and gold threads

One of the oldest forms of weaponry, the bow long remained in use in the East. A special case (*naluch*) held the bow, and together with the quiver for the arrows, it made up the so-called *saadak* set, or simply a *saadak*.

In the sixteenth century the *saadak* was the main weapon used by the Russian gentry militia, but it was largely replaced by firearms in the next century. It was retained as a fighting weapon in sentry detachments and in national units made up of troops from the country's eastern regions. It also continued to be utilized for hunting.

The Armory has preserved several valuable *saadak*s that were displayed during grand ceremonies and military reviews. This *saadak* entered the Armory in 1736 from the Stable Treasury, an office of the imperial court that took the place of the Stable Office. The leather quiver and bow case are covered in velvet and embroidered with gold and silver thread. Ottoman motifs are clearly discernible in the floral design of large carnations on slender stems. Silver appliqués and buckles on belts with a niello plant design further embellish the opulent decoration.

61. STIKHARION (SURPLICE) YOKE

Russia, mid-17th century; silk (altabas): Turkey, 17th century;
embroidery: Russia, mid-17th century
Silk, canvas, gold, silver, precious gems, pearls

Gold openwork plaques of fantastic shapes, recalling various southern flowers and adorned with precious stones and colored enamel, complement the pearl embroidery on the yoke of this stikharion, or deacon's surplice (see next page). Embroidered with large pearls on a gold fabric ground is a design of plant scrolls that extends symmetrically from enameled plaques set with diamonds, emeralds, and rubies. A row of small square openwork plaques runs along the edge.

It was common practice in seventeenth-century Russian life to preserve fragments of costly materials and imported fabrics made of gold and silver threads, as well as high-quality embroideries, gems and pearls, and metal plaques and appliqué. Particularly treasured were items that once belonged to members of the tsar's family or were commissioned by them from the Kremlin workshops. To judge by the luxurious materials and exceptional execution, this stikharion yoke is undoubtedly one such piece. The material used in its construction most likely came from the Tsar's Treasury. This was the only storage area that housed large quantities of gold plaques inset with precious stones that were brought from Turkey as diplomatic gifts. Such plaques were used to create ceremonial garb and objects, along with items the tsar donated to the sacristies of the Kremlin churches and cathedrals. The embroidery was completed in the Tsarina's Chamber of the Kremlin workshops.

62. SAKKOS

Embroidery: Moscow, after 1658; satin body: Turkey, late 16th–early 17th century; satin front panel: Istanbul, 1670s
Gilded satin, velvet, taffeta, gold and silver spun thread, braid, silver

As the most ceremonial vestment worn by high-ranking members of the clergy of the Orthodox church, the sakkos derives its theological symbolism from the "purple mantle of Christ." This sakkos is a long garment that is open at the sides with short, wide sleeves (see page 12). It also has a round yoke, cuffs, borders on the sides and along the bottom, and a *napersnik* or *naramnik* (a narrow vertical strip in the center front) that was added in the mid-seventeenth century. Until the 1670s only the Moscow metropolitans and patriarchs, as the heads of the Russian church, could rightfully wear a sakkos to celebrate the liturgy. All of their luxurious vestments were made with exceptional skill. As stated in early documents, a sakkos was constructed from imported expensive fabrics of the very highest artistic quality. Individual parts of the sakkos with specific connotations were generally designated by the use of a different fabric and were embellished with embroidery (ornamental or pictorial), gold and silver plaques, pearls, and precious gems. After the death of a sakkos's owner, his vestment became the property of the Russian church and was transferred for safekeeping to the Patriarchal Sacristy. This celebrated storehouse for the prized possessions of the Russian Orthodox church is permanently located within the Moscow Kremlin.

Patriarch Iosif, a contemporary of Tsar Mikhail Fedorovich and Tsar Alexei Mikhailovich, once owned this sakkos made of gold fabric, called *ob'iar'* in Russian. Intersecting ribbons form a pattern of large and small circles. Four-point crosses with figured ends, the monogram of Christ, and the inscription NIKA fill the large circles, while the smaller ones contain four-point crosses that widen at the ends. Cherubim occupy the space between the ribbon loops. The design is woven with spun gold thread on a red ground. A fabric with a similar pattern was mentioned as being among the wares that the Russian ambassadors Afanasei Pronchishchev and Tikhon Ermolov brought from Istanbul in 1633.

The front section of the sakkos consists of blue satin with a woven image of Christ enthroned and flanked by symbols of the Four Evangelists. For a long time the origins of this fabric were not clearly established. M. N. Levinson-Nechaeva, former curator of the Kremlin Museums' Department of Fabrics in the 1920s and 1930s, noted the combination of two different decorative styles that are "post-Byzantine in the pictorial images" and "purely Iranian in the treatment of the plant elements."[54] Later publications attributed the fabric to the court workshops of the sultan in Istanbul.[55] The sakkos of Metropolitan Dionisii, one of two made in accordance with a decree issued by Tsar Ivan the Terrible in 1583, was sewn from the same satin (Kremlin Museums, inv. no. TK-12). The creation of these vestments was linked to tragic events in the Rurik dynasty. In 1581 Tsar Ivan's eldest son, the twenty-seven-year-old Tsarevich Ivan, died, as contemporaries believed, at his father's hand. The sakkoses of Metropolitan Dionisii became a material "memorial" to a father and tsar who lost both his son and the heir to the throne.

Fabric pieces left over from the creation of these sakkoses were long preserved in the Tsar's Treasury. Some time later a small piece of blue satin woven with the image of Christ enthroned was incorporated into the front panel of the sakkos of Patriarch Iosif. This addition was one restoration made to the vestment, as noted in the 1658 inventory of the Sacristy.[56] Another repair, linked with the replacement of the original yoke and cuffs, occurred some time between the compilation of the 1658 inventory and the following one of 1675, in which the current state of the vestment is described.[57] Patterns that copy Ottoman woven designs are embroidered with spun gold thread on the black velvet of the yoke and cuffs (see above). Moreover, the gilded pattern on the yoke is partly cut and thus leaves large parts of the ground visible, in imitation of patterned gilded black velvet. On the cuffs the embroidered pattern is so dense that the ground is seen only around the outlines, as in patterned brocade. The lining of the sakkos is made from plain green taffeta.

123

63. TABERNACLE

Russia (plaques), Moscow (tabernacle), first quarter 18th century
Gold, silver, precious gems, stones, river pearls

A tabernacle is used in Orthodox rites for storing sacramental bread and wine (symbols of the body and blood of Christ) and for administering the sacraments to the faithful. This one takes the form of a traditional Russian five-domed church. Depicted on its front is the Crucifixion, with the Mother of God and John the Baptist, as well as the instruments of the Passion — the speaar and sponge — on either side, and the Holy Ghost above the cross. Six medallions arranged around the Crucifixion contain scenes of the Passion of Christ (clockwise from lower left): the Bearing of the Cross, the Crowning with Thorns, the Flagellation, the Pentecost, the Kiss of Judas, and Christ before Pilate. On the sides are depictions of the Eucharist (see left). Figures of the Evangelists and four removable compartments for the Eucharistic bread are on the reverse of the tabernacle.

Early descriptions of this tabernacle, preserved in documents from the first quarter of the eighteenth century, indicate its current appearance does not fully correspond to its original one. Four gold wings with niello depictions of archangels, now removed, were initially affixed to its upper section. In addition, the tabernacle formerly was attached to a rectangular silver base, which is now missing.

Both the form of the object and the numerous depictions of saints and scenes from the New Testament associated with the symbolic role of the tabernacle make its conceptual significance exceptionally rich and multilayered. Moreover, its material and artistic value elevate it to one of the most significant examples of the Moscow jeweler's art from the early eighteenth century.

More than 2.5 kilograms of gold and an abundance of precious stones — rubies, emeralds, and sapphires — decorate the tabernacle. In the upper section a gold cross is affixed to an enormous pink tourmaline that weighs 129 grams. This cross and tourmaline in the shape of a mountain specifically allude to Golgotha, the site of the Crucifixion. The figurative and narrative compositions benefit from exceptionally effective techniques, such as niello, enamel over an engraved gold ground, and painted enamel. Western European engravings served as iconographic prototypes for many of these scenes. The treatment of the gold medallions set with precious stones, particularly the two in the form of pomegranates on the side panels, were clearly inspired by Ottoman art. Perhaps these medallions came to Russia from the Ottoman Empire. It is also possible that they were actually made in Russia in the Kremlin workshops, which were international both in their complement of workmen and in the creative spirit reigning there.

64. PLAQUE (PANAGIA)

Turkey, Istanbul, second half 17th century
Gold, emeralds, diamonds, rubies

Dominating the center of the plaque is an enormous rose-cut emerald set in a petal-shaped mount. It is bordered with table-cut rubies and table- and rose-cut diamonds in mounts shaped like stylized leaves or flowers. Above this is an equal-sided cross of diamonds. Foil placed beneath the colored stones makes them sparkle brightly. The back of the plaque is covered with a fine plant design executed in carved relief (see above).

Objects with Christian symbols constituted a prominent part of the production of Greek jewelers and silversmiths as well as weavers from the Orthodox diaspora of the Ottoman Empire. They were intended for domestic use by the local Christian population and for export to Christian countries, especially to Russia. Thus, it was not unusual that "an image of the most pure Hodigitria Mother of God, carved of jasper, edged in gold with rubies and emeralds" was given to Patriarch Filaret by Thomas Cantacuzene, the Greek head of the Ottoman embassy, in 1627.[58] Three years later Cantacuzene presented as part of his personal gifts to Tsar Mikhail Fedorovich and his son and heir, Tsarevich Alexei Mikhailovich, a gold cross "with diamonds and red spinels." He also offered two panagias to Patriarch Filaret. One was "a piece of white jasper on which the Annunciation of the Mother of God is carved . . ."; the other was "a piece of white jasper carved with the Ascension of Christ. . . ." Each had a gold frame decorated with precious stones.[59]

In 1633 the "Turk" and Muslim Mustafa Beg, a member of the embassy of Ali-Agi, presented an unexpected gift to Tsar Mikhail Fedorovich — a saber and "a cross, with a ruby set in gold bordered with red spinels and rubies." A more detailed description was recorded in the Treasury Office: "a gold fish, on it a cross with the Crucifixion of the Lord, with rubies and red spinels and emeralds on the fish."[60] A member of the next Ottoman embassy of 1634–1636, a Greek known as Ondronik in the Russian documents, presented Tsar Mikhail Fedorovich with a panagia that was "gold, with a stone of chalcedony carved with an image of the Archangel Michael, and edged with ruby chips." From that same embassy Tsarevich Alexei Mikhailovich received gifts from Archimandrite Amphilochius, among them costly fabrics, clothing, and "a cross . . . gold with diamonds, the Crucifixion of our Lord applied in niello."[61] At other times such wares were acquired from visiting Greek merchants. In 1656, for example, two panagias, though without carved biblical scenes in the center, were purchased from Dmitry Konstantinov, including "a gold panagia with niello on gold, a cross and beneath the cross a sapphire, in the cross and near it diamonds and rubies, on the bottom edge on wire shanks three emeralds" and "a gold panagia with diamonds and rubies, two sapphires, and two red spinels on shanks."[62] This plaque, which once had special suspension rings, conceivably could have been used as a panagia at one time.

65. PECTORAL ICON (PANAGIA)

Turkey, Istanbul, first half 17th century
Silver, gold, precious gems

This panagia is an oval, openwork plate with a figured edge decorated with a plant design of stylized scrolling stems with shoots. The silver stems, embellished with green enamel leaves and rose-cut diamonds, end in table-cut rubies set in leaf-shaped mounts. A square sapphire carved with an image of Jesus Christ in a leaf-shaped mount framed with rubies anchors the center.

Above the sapphire is a cross of rose-cut diamonds. An imperial crown tops the panagia, and three silver pendants set with rubies,

emeralds, and diamonds dangle below it. Headpieces in the shape of imperial crowns were not added to panagias until after the 1720s, when Tsar Petr Alexevich adopted the title of emperor. Technical details, such as the form of the cast and the fastening of the stones, indicate the pendants were added to this panagia at the same time as the imperial crown.

PAGE 3, FIGURE 2. SEAL RING
Golden Horde, 14th century
Copper, semiprecious stone
Casting, stone engraving
Diam. 2.7 cm
From the Patriarchal Sacristy
Inv. no. MV-26

1. ICON OF MOTHER OF GOD GALAKTOTROPHOUSA
Painting: Moscow, 16th century; *oklad*: repoussé, Golden Horde or Russia, 14th century; plaques, Russia, late 14th–early 15th century; crowns, Moscow, late 14th–early 15th century
Gold, silver, pearls, precious stones, wood
Repoussé, chasing, filigree, enamel, tempera
L. 52.2 cm; W. 40 cm
From the Novodevichy Convent, Moscow; entered the Armory in 1927
Inv. no. Zh-1760/1–2

SOURCES: Inventory of Novodevichy Monastery, 1861, l. 103.

LITERATURE: Marytnova 1984, pp. 101–12; Zolotaia Orda 2005, cat. 530, ill. on p. 16.

2. PHELONION
Gilded satin: territories of the Ottoman Empire, Damascus (?), 16th century; sewing: Russia, mid-16th century; plaques: Golden Horde, 14th century, Moscow, 16th–17th century
Gilded satin, satin, sackcloth, silver, gold thread, pearls, copper
Weaving, sewing, repoussé, gilding
L. 145 cm
From the Protection of the Virgin (Pokrovsky) Convent, Suzdal
Transferred from the Vladimir Regional Museum in 1931
Inv. no. TK-2434
Published here for the first time.

SOURCES: Opis' Oruzheinoi palaty 1914–1930, ll. 56, 56ob, no. 18853.

3. WIDE COLLAR
Iran, 15th century
Silk and cotton fabrics, spun gold and silver threads, silk thread
Weaving, sewing
H. 154 cm; W. 93 cm
From the Main Collection of the Armory
Inv. no. TK-3117

SOURCES: Opis' Oruzheinoi palaty 1808, vol. 2, l. 224; Opis' Oruzheinoi palaty 1835; Opis' Oruzheinoi palaty 1884–1893, ch. 2, kn. 3, no. 3685.

LITERATURE: Martin 1899, p. 15; Die Ausstellung 1910, plate 206; A Survey of Persian Art 1964, vol. 3, pp. 2078, 2157, plate 1017; Sokrovishcha Irana i Turtsii 1979, cat. 32; Timur and the Princely Vision 1989, p. 217, cat. 116.

4. COVERLET FOR THE TSAR'S THRONE
Embroidery: Iran, first half 17th century; execution: Moscow, Kremlin workshops, 17th century
Velvet, canvas, gold thread, silk thread, *naboika*
Weaving, embroidery
L. 195 cm; W. 72 (central section), 129 cm (including wings)
From the Main Collection of the Armory
Inv. no. TK-2195

SOURCES: Opis' Oruzheinoi palaty 1884–1893, ch. 2, kn. 3, no. 3685.

LITERATURE: Sokrovishcha Irana i Turtsii 1979, cat. 33.

5. SHIELD
Iran (Qazvin?), 16th century; master: Muhammad Mumin
Watered steel, gold, rubies, pearls, turquoise, fabric, fringe
Forging, chasing, carving, damascening, filigree, gilding, silvering, flat chasing
Diam. 48.8 cm
From the Main Collection of the Armory
Inv. no. OR-176

SOURCES: Perepisnaia kniga Oruzhenoi kazne 1686/1687, p. 186; Opis' Oruzheinoi palaty 1884–1893, ch. 2, kn. 2, no. 5067.

LITERATURE: Mishukov 1954, pp. 123, 124; Gosudareva Oruzheinaia palata 2002, no. 31, ill. on p. 129; Oruzheinaia palata 2006, no. 183, pp. 214–16; The Arsenal 2007, pp. 7–8; Vera i vlast' 2007, cat. 19.

6, 7. SABER BLADES
Iran, Isfahan, first half 17th century; master: Rajab-Ali Isfahani
Watered steel
Forging, damascening
L. 99.3 cm, 97.5 cm; W. of blades near heel 3.1 cm
From the Main Collection of the Armory
Inv. nos. OR-1413, OR-772

SOURCES: Perepisnaia kniga Oruzheinoi

kazne 1686/1687, l. 62, no. 3, 6; Opis' Oruzheinoi palaty 1884–1893, ch. 4, kn. 3, nos. 6085, 6086.

LITERATURE: The Arsenal 2007, pp. 47–48.

8. HELMET WITH MASK
Iran, 16th century
Steel
Forging, engraving, gilding
Diam. 22.5 cm; Weight 1300 g
From the Main Collection of the Armory
Inv. no. OR-2056

SOURCES: Opis' Oruzheinoi palaty 1884–1893, ch. 3, kn. 2, no. 4405.

LITERATURE: Gosudareva Oruzheinaia palata 2002, nos. 10, 11.

9. HANGING
Iran, mid-17th century
Brocade
Weaving
H. 169 cm; W. 128 cm
From the Main Collection of the Armory
Inv. no. TK-3126

SOURCES: Opis' koniushennym veshcham 1706, l. 306ob.; Opis' Oruzheinoi palaty 1884–1893, ch. 6, kn. 5, p. 128, no. 8860.

LITERATURE: Martin 1899, p. 15, Die Ausstellung 1910, vol. 3, plate 204; A Survey of Persian Art 1964, vol. 3, p. 2136, plate 1055B; Levinson-Nechaeva 1954, p. 345; Denisova 1954, p. 278; Pirverdian 1971, p. 4; Sokrovishcha Irana i Turtsii 1979, cat. 35; Vishnevskaya 2007, cat. 6.

10. SADDLE BLANKET
Russia, Kremlin workshops, 17th century; velvet centerpiece: Iran, early 17th century; damask border: Italy, 17th century
Taffeta, velvet, silk
Weaving
L. 143 cm; W. 120 cm
From the Main Collection of the Armory
Inv. no. TK-2200

SOURCES: Opis' Oruzheinoi palaty 1884–1893, ch. 6, kn. 5, no. 8868.

LITERATURE: Putevoditel' 1960, ill. 2; Oruzheinaia palata 1964, ill. on p. 310; Gosudardstvennaia Oruzheinaia palata 1969, ill. 136; Sokrovishcha Irana i Turtsii 1979, p. 29, no. 40; Vishnevskaya 2007, cat. 4.

11. CAPARISON

Iran, early 17th century; additions: Moscow, Kremlin workshops, 17th century
Cloth, gold and silk threads
Weaving, embroidery
H. 118 cm; W. 127 cm
From the Main Collection of the Armory
Inv. no. TK-2205

SOURCES: Opis' Oruzheinoi palaty 1884–1893, ch. 6, kn. 5, no. 9123.

LITERATURE: Denisova 1954, p. 278, ill. 25; Oruzheinaia palata 1964, ill. 136; Sokrovishcha Irana i Turtsii 1979, p. 26, no. 26; Mironova 1996, p. 183, ill. 153; Gifts to the Tsars 2001, p. 195, no. 40; "Vo utverzhdenie druzhby . . ." 2005, pp. 86–87, no. 44; The Arsenal 2007, pp. 41–42.

12. BROADSWORD AND SCABBARD

Iran, before 1645
Steel, gold, precious stones, nephrite, velvet, braid
Forging, carving, encrustation, enamel, engraving, oxidation, gilding, chasing, flat chasing
Overall L. 91 cm; L. of blade 78 cm
From the Main Collection of the Armory
Inv. no. OR 4443/1–3

SOURCES: Perepisnaia kniga Oruzheinoi kazne 1686–1687, l. 76; Opis' Oruzheinoi palaty 1884–1893, ch. 4, kn. 3, no. 5702.

LITERATURE: Gosudareva Oruzheinaia palata 2002, no. 46; The Arsenal 2007, pp. 39–40.

13. SABER AND SCABBARD

Iran, first half 17th century
Steel, wood, gold, silver, jasper, precious stones, braid
Forging, carving, repoussé, niello, encrustation, damascening, enamel
Overall L. 101 cm; L. of blade 89 cm
From the Main Collection of the Armory
Inv. no. OR-197/1–3

SOURCES: Perepisnaia kniga Oruzheinoi kazne 1686/1687, l. 30; Rospis' pokhodnoi kazny 1654–1655, l. 88; Opis' Oruzheinoi palaty 1884–1893, ch. 4, kn. 3, no. 5907.

LITERATURE: Arsenal of the Russian Tsars 1998, cat. 36; Orel i lev 2001, cat. 200; Gosudareva Oruzheinaia palata 2002, no. 39.

14. CEREMONIAL MACE

Iran, mid-17th century
Gold, wood, turquoise
Carving, encrustation
L. 52 cm
From the Main Collection of the Armory
Inv. no. OR-187

SOURCES: Perepisnaia kniga Oruzheinoi kazne 1686/1687, l. 116, no. 1; Opis' Oruzheinoi palaty 1884–1893, ch. 4, kn. 3, no. 5241.

LITERATURE: Arsenal of the Russian Tsars 1998, cat. 33; Gifts to the Tsars 2001, cat. 43; Gosudareva Oruzheinaia palata 2002, no. 56; "Vo utverzhdenie druzhby . . ." 2005, cat. 46.

15. DAGGER AND SHEATH

Iran, first half 17th century
Steel, wood, gold, rubies, turquoise, pearls
Forging, carving, repoussé, filigree, chasing
L. 30.8 cm; L. of blade 16.8 cm
From the Main Collection of the Armory
Inv. no. OR-208/1–2

SOURCES: Prikhodnaia kniga 1616–1617, l. 34; Opis' Oruzheinoi palaty 1884–1893, ch. 4, kn. 3, no. 6169.

LITERATURE: Gosudareva Oruzheinaia palata 2002, p. 348, no. 50; Yablonskaya 1996, p. 95, no. 90, fig. 90; Gifts to the Tsars 2001, p. 193, cat. 38; "Vo utverzhdenie druzhby . . ." 2005, cat. 40, p. 82; Oruzheinaia palata 2006, p. 216.

16. HORN

Gift of the States General of the Dutch Republic to Tsar Alexei Mikhailovich in 1665
Iran, first half 17th century
Buffalo horn, gold, precious and semiprecious stones, glass, enamel
Casting, chasing, punching
L. 41 cm
From the Main Collection of the Armory
Inv. no. DK-263

SOURCES: Posol'skaia kniga 1664–1665, ll, 89, 97ob, 142; Opis' Oruzheinoi palaty 1884–1893, ch. 2, kn. 3, no. 229.

LITERATURE: Drevnosti 1853, otd. 5, p. 45, fig. 31; Savvaitov 1865, p. 72; Vishnevskaya 1996, vol. 2, p. 199, no. 166; "Vo utverzhdenie druzhby . . ." 2005, cat. 31, p. 74.

17. STAFF

Gift of Shah Abbas I of Iran to Patriarch Filaret in 1629
Iran, late 16th–early 17th century; additions: Russia, first third 17th century
Wood, gold, precious and semiprecious stones, glass
Casting, repoussé, flat chasing
L. 150 cm
Transferred from the Patriarchal Sacristy in 1920
Inv. no. DK-840

SOURCES: Opis' keleinoi kazny 1876, pp. 912–13; Savva 1883, p. 30, no. 1, tab. 10, no. 49; Opis' Oruzheinoi palaty 1914–1930, f. 1, op. 3, d. 12, no. 11011.

LITERATURE: "Vo utverzhdenie druzhby . . ." 2005, cat. 41, p. 83; Vishnevskaya 1996, vol. 2, pp. 206–207, illus. 172–73.

18. BRIDLE

Gift of Shah Safi of Iran to Tsar Mikhail Fedorovich in 1641
Iran, first half 17th century
Gold, silver, rubies, emeralds, turquoise, leather
Casting, repoussé
L. 60 cm
From the Main Collection of the Armory
Inv. no. K-1015

SOURCES: Posol'skaia kniga 1640–1643, ll. 189ob–193ob, 232; Opis' koniushennym

veshcham 1706, ll. 3–3ob; Opis' Oruzheinoi palaty 1884–1893, ch. 6, kn. 5, no. 8625.

LITERATURE: Denisova 1954, p. 278; Sokrovishcha Irana i Turtsii 1979, no. 25; Melnikova 2004, pp. 205–206; "Vo utverzhdenie druzhby . . ." 2005, no. 42.

19. SADDLE

Russia, Kremlin workshops, second half 17th century; velvet: Iran, 17th century
Silver, wood, velvet, leather
Carving, gilding, weaving
L. 44 cm; H. of front pommel 26.5 cm; H. of cantle 20 cm
From the Main Collection of the Armory
Inv. no. K-506

SOURCES: Opis' koniushennym veshcham 1706, archaki, no. 121, l. 198; Opis' Oruzheinoi palaty 1884–1893, ch. 6, kn. 5, no. 8484.

LITERATURE: Sokrovishcha Irana i Turtsii 1979, cat. 30.

20. CHAIN-MAIL SHIRT

Turkey, 17th century
Steel
Forging, riveting, damascening
L. 72 cm; Weight 14,800 g
From the Main Collection of the Armory
Inv. no. OR-32

SOURCES: Rospis' pokhodnoi kazny 1654–1656, l. 43; Perepisnaia kniga Oruzheinoi kazne 1686/1687, l. 509; Opis' Oruzheinoi palaty 1884–1893, ch. 3, kn. 2, no. 4561.

LITERATURE: Gosudareva Oruzheinaia palata 2002, cat. 19; Iskusstvo Porty 2008, cat. 7.

21. HELMET

Turkey, late 16th–early 17th century
Watered steel, silver, silk fabric
Forging, chasing, carving, damascening
Diam. 22 cm
From the Main Collection of the Armory
Inv. no. OR-163

SOURCES: Perepisnaia kniga Oruzheinoi kazne 1686/1687, l. 461, no. 2; Rospis' pokhodnoi kazny 1654–1655, no. 4; Opis' Oruzheinoi palaty 1884–1893, ch. 3, kn. 2, no. 4412.

LITERATURE: Yablonskaya 1996, pp. 100–101, no. 93; Tesoros 1990, cat. 90; Orel i lev 2001, cat. 195; Gosudareva Oruzheinaia palata 2002, no. 8; Chevaux 2002, cat. 110; The Arsenal 2007, pp. 1–2.

22. CAPARISON

Russia, Kremlin workshops, 17th century; gilded satin: Turkey, mid-16th century
Gilded satin, satin, taffeta
Weaving
Diam. 188 cm
From the Main Collection of the Armory
Inv. no. TK-2201

SOURCES: Opis' Tsaria Ivana Vasil'evicha 1850; Opis' Oruzheinoi palaty 1884–1893, ch. 6, kn. 5, no. 8943.

LITERATURE: Levinson-Nechaeva 1954, p. 348; Sokrovishcha Irana i Turtsii 1979, cat. 106; Vishnevskaya 2007, cat. 14, pp. 56–57; Iskusstvo Porty 2008, cat. 73.

23. DAGGER AND SHEATH
Turkey, second half 16th century; blade: Iran, 16th century; master: Mahmud, son of Mas'ud
Steel, nephrite, gold, diamonds, rubies
Forging, carving, enamel, damascening, encrustation, gilding
Overall L. 31 cm; L. of blade 20 cm; L. of sheath 23 cm
From the Main Collection of the Armory
Inv. no. OR-210/1–2

SOURCES: Opis' oruzhiia 1810, no. 23; Opis' Oruzheinoi palaty 1884–1893, ch. 4, kn. 3, no. 6171.

LITERATURE: Imperatorskaia Riust-kamera 2004, cat. 94; Iskusstvo Porty 2008, cat. 18.

24. SABER AND SCABBARD OF THE GRAND ATTIRE
Turkey, before 1656
Watered steel, wood, gold, emeralds, rubies, sapphires, nephrite
Forging, carving, niello, encrustation, damascening
Overall L. 94 cm; L. of blade 81.5 cm
From the Main Collection of the Armory
Inv. no. OR-199/1–2

SOURCES: Perepisnaia kniga Oruzheinoi kazne 1686/1687, l. 27; Opis' Oruzheinoi palaty 1884–1893, ch. 4, kn. 3, no. 5909.

LITERATURE: Gifts to the Tsars 2001, cat. 34; "Vo utverzhdenie druzhby . . ." 2005, cat. 65; The Arsenal 2007, pp. 35–36; Iskusstvo Porty 2008, cat. 9.

25. FLASK
Gift of Tsarevich Seid-Burkhan Arsalanovich to Tsar Alexei Mikhailovich in 1653
Turkey, first half 17th century
Leather, silver cannetille, nephrite, rubies, emeralds, glass, gold, silver, rock crystal
Embroidery, carved relief, niello, gilding
H. 27.5 cm; W. 21.5 cm
From the Main Collection of the Armory
Inv. no. TK-2882

SOURCES: Opis' 1663–1666, l. 200; Opis' 1676, l. 20; Opis' Oruzheinoi palaty 1835, no. 2500; Opis' Oruzheinoi palaty 1884–1893, no. 2764.

LITERATURE: Iskusstvo Porty 2008, cat. 36.

26. CEREMONIAL MACE
Turkey, Istanbul, mid-17th century
Gold, wood, garnets, emeralds, rubies, enamel
Carving, chasing
L. 69 cm
From the Main Collection of the Armory
Inv. no. OR-184

SOURCES: Rospis' pokhodnoi kazny 1654–1655, l. 7; Perepisnaia kniga Oruzheinoi kazne 1686/1687, l. 113; Opis' Oruzheinoi palaty 1884–1893, ch. 4, kn. 3, no. 5226.

LITERATURE: Yablonskaya 1996, p. 96; Rossiiskie imperatory 2006, cat. 89; Iskusstvo Porty 2008, cat. 20.

27. CEREMONIAL SHIELD
Turkey, mid-17th century
Cane, steel, gold, gold and silk threads, rubies, turquoise, velvet, braid
Carving, chasing, damascening, repoussé
Diam. 48.5 cm
From the Main Collection of the Armory
Inv. no. OR-174

SOURCES: Perepisnaia kniga Oruzheinoi kazne 1686/1687, l. 190; Opis' Oruzheinoi palaty 1884–1893, ch. 3, kn. 2, no. 5064.

LITERATURE: Alexander 1992, p. 120, no. 67; Chevaux 2002, cat. 111; Iskusstvo Porty 2008, cat. 8.

28. CURTAIN
Russia, 17th century; velvet, Turkey, first half 17th century
Raised-pile gilded velvet, gilded fringe
Weaving
H. 165 cm; W. 128 cm (without fringe)
From the Main Collection of the Armory
Inv. no. TK-2685

SOURCES: Opis' tsarskoi kazny 1640, l. 331 ob; Opis' Oruzheinoi palaty 1884–1893, ch. 2, kn. 3, no. 3722.

LITERATURE: Putevoditel' 1960, fig. 30; Sokrovishcha Irana i Turtsii 1979, cat. 148, p. 54; Vishnevskaya 2007, cat. 29; Iskusstvo Porty 2008, cat. 81.

29. CAPARISON
Turkey, late 17th century
Brocade, fringe, dyed homespun
Weaving, braiding
H. 158 cm; W. 151 cm
From the Main Collection of the Armory
Inv. no. TK-2202

SOURCES: Opis' Oruzheinoi palaty 1884–1893, ch. 6, kn. 5, no. 8951.

LITERATURE: The Arsenal 2007, pp. 65–66.

30. SAADAK COVER
Russia, 17th century; center panel: Turkey, first half 17th century; border: Iran, first half 17th century
Embossed gilded velvet, taffeta, fringe
Weaving
H. 150 cm; W. 120 cm
From the Main Collection of the Armory
Inv. no. TK-2682

SOURCES: Perepisnaia kniga Oruzheinoi kazne 1686/1687, l. 162; Opis' Oruzheinoi palaty 1835, ch. 4, p. 555, no. 5480; Opis' Oruzheinoi palaty 1884–1893, ch. 4, kn. 3, no. 6358.

LITERATURE: Sokrovishcha Irana i Turtsii 1979, p. 31, no. 43; Vishnevskaya 1996, pp. 232–33, no. 194, 195; Vishnevskaya 2007, no. 31, pp. 90–91.

31. SADDLECLOTH
Turkey, 17th century
Velvet, silk, gold threads
Sewing, weaving
H. 70 cm; W. 130 cm
From the Main Collection of the Armory
Inv. no. TK-586

SOURCES: Opis' Oruzheinoi palaty 1884–1893, op. 6, kn. 5, no. 9128.

LITERATURE: Denisova 1954, pp. 278–79; The Arsenal 2007, pp. 55–56.

32. SADDLE
Turkey, mid-17th century
Gold, silver, gold thread, rubies, emeralds, pearls, wood, leather, velvet, braid
Chasing, embroidery, weaving, gilding
H. of front pommel 32 cm; L. of saddle 40 cm
From the Main Collection of the Armory
Inv. no. K-229

SOURCES: Opis' koniushennym veshcham 1706, ll. 140–140ob; Opis' Oruzheinoi palaty 1886, ch. 6, kn. 5, no. 8522.

LITERATURE: Kologrivov 1911, pp. 148–51; Mironova 1996, pp. 159–69; Treasures 1996, no. 80; Arsenal of the Russian Tsars 1998, cat. 7; Gifts to the Tsars 2001, cat. 2; The Arsenal 2007, pp. 53–54.

33. PAIR OF STIRRUPS
Turkey, mid-17th century
Gold, rubies, emeralds, iron, velvet, gold thread
Chasing, enamel, carving, gilding, weaving, embroidery
H. each 16.5 cm
From the Main Collection of the Armory
Inv. no. K-216/1–2

SOURCES: Opis' koniushennym veshcham 1706, no. 98, l. 189; Opis' Oruzheinoi palaty 1884–1893, ch. 6, kn. 5, no. 8425.

LITERATURE: Splendeur 1993, p. 23; Treasures 1996, cat. 82; Gifts to the Tsars 2001, no. 32; The Arsenal 2007, pp. 57–58; Iskusstvo Porty 2008, cat. 24.

34. PAIR OF STIRRUPS
Turkey, mid-17th century
Iron, gold, pearls, rubies, emeralds, fabric, gold thread
Forging, gilding, chasing, weaving, embroidery
H. each 16.5 cm
From the Main Collection of the Armory
Inv. no. K-217/1–2

SOURCES: Opis' koniushennym veshcham 1706, ll. 193ob–194; Kopii s ukazov 1721–1731, l. 22; Opis' Oruzheinoi palaty 1884–1893, ch. 6, kn. 5, no. 8726.

LITERATURE: Iskusstvo Porty 2008, cat. 25.

35, 36. BRIDLE AND CHEST STRAPS
Turkey, before 1622/1623
Gold, silver, rubies, pearls, turquoise,
nephrite, leather, braid
Gilding, chasing, encrustation
W. of straps 3.5 cm, 4 cm
From the Main Collection of the Armory
Inv. no. K-293, K-294

SOURCES: Opis' koniushennym veshcham
1706, ll. 68–68ob; Opis' Oruzheinoi palaty
1884–1893, ch. 6, kn. 5, no. 8690.

LITERATURE: Denisova 1954, pp. 284, 288;
Mironova 1996, p. 154 (illus.); Sokrovishcha
Irana i Turtsii 1979, cat. 112–13.

37, 38. BRIDLE AND CHEST STRAPS
Turkey, 17th century
Leather, silver, rubies, emeralds, turquoise,
nephrite, silk, braid
Gilding, carving, niello, encrustation,
chasing, weaving
Bridle: L. of straps 151 cm, 110 cm; W. of
straps 5 cm
Chest straps: L. 65 cm; W. 6.5 cm
From the Main Collection of the Armory
Inv. nos. K-996, K-995

SOURCES: Opis' koniushennym veshcham
1706, ll. 80–80ob.; Opis' Oruzheinoi palaty
1884–1893, ch. 6, kn. 5, no. 8698; Rospis'
Romanova 1887, p. 50.

LITERATURE: Schätze 1991, nos. 58, 59;
Treasures 1996, nos. 72, 73; Chevaux 2002,
no. 109; Iskusstvo Porty 2008, cats. 30, 31.

**39, 40, 41. BRIDLE, CHEST STRAPS,
AND CRUPPER**
Presented by Ambassador Rusan Beg of Iran
to Tsar Mikhail Fedorovich in 1624/1625
Turkey, before 1625
Braid, leather, gold, silver, rubies, turquoise,
peridots
Niello, carving, chasing, weaving
L. of bridle 58 cm; L. of chest straps 62, 62, 15
cm; L. of crupper 115 cm; W. of straps 4.5 cm
From the Main Collection of the Armory
Inv. nos. K-283, K-284, K-285

SOURCES: Dela Persidskogo dvora 1618–1624,
l. 2; Opis' koniushennym veshcham 1706,
ll. 1ob–2; Opis' Oruzheinoi palaty 1835, no.
3668; Opis' Oruzheinoi palaty 1884–1893, ch.
6, kn. 5, no. 8621.

LITERATURE: Kologrivov 1911, p. 79; Denisova
1954, pp. 276, 284; Kirillova 1964, p. 309;
Mironova 1996, pp. 188–89; Sokrovishcha
Irana i Turtsii 1979, cat. 109–11, p. 46;
Remekmuvek 1989, cat. 19; Tesoros 1990,
cat. 28–30.

42. BOWL
Gift of Georgios Panagiotis to Tsar Mikhail
Fedorovich in 1632
Turkey, first third 17th century
Nephrite, gold, emeralds, rubies, sapphires
Carving, encrustation
H. 12.2 cm; Diam. 14.5 cm

From the Main Collection of the Armory
Inv. no. DK-267

SOURCES: Prikhodnaia kniga 1631–1632, ll.
42–42ob; Opis' tsarskoi kazny 1634, l. 36;
Opis' Oruzheinoi palaty 1835, no. 2407; Opis'
Oruzheinoi palaty 1884–1893, ch. 2, kn. 3,
no. 2506.

LITERATURE: Drevnosti 1853, otd. 5, tab.
15; Viktorov 1877, p. 12; Kologrivov 1911,
pp. 99–100; Putevoditel' 1960, p. 10, ill. 19;
Vishnevskaya 1996, pp. 218–19, ill. 181; Gifts
to the Tsars 2001, cat. 30; "Vo utverzhdenie
druzhby . . ." 2005, cat. 62; Iskusstvo Porty
2008, cat. 39.

43. TANKARD
Gift of Patriarch Cyril I Lukaris to Tsar
Mikhail Fedorovich in 1632
Turkey, first third 17th century
Rock crystal, gold, rubies, emeralds
Carving, encrustation
H. 15.5 cm
From the Main Collection of the Armory
Inv. no. DK-82

SOURCES: Posol'skie dela 1631–1632, l. 361;
Prikhodnaia kniga 1631–1632, l. 41; Opis'
tsarskoi kazny 1634, l. 377; Opis' Oruzheinoi
palaty 1884–1893, ch. 2, kn. 1, no. 534.

LITERATURE: Viktorov 1877, p. 12; Putevoditel'
1960, p. 10, ill. 18; Vishnevskaya 1996, pp.
220–21, ill. 182; Gifts to the Tsars 2001, no.
22; "Vo utverzhdenie druzhby . . ." 2005, cat.
55; Iskusstvo Porty 2008, cat. 41.

44. BOWL
Turkey, Istanbul, 17th century
Agate, gold, rubies, emeralds, rock crystal
Carving, encrustation, engraving
H. 4.5 cm; Diam. 9 cm
From the Main Collection of the Armory
Inv. no. DK-265

SOURCES: Opis' Oruzheinoi palaty 1835,
no. 2517; Opis' Oruzheinoi palaty 1884–
1893, ch. 2, kn. 3, no. 2498.

LITERATURE: Gifts to the Tsars 2001, no. 30;
"Vo utverzhdenie druzhby . . ." 2005, no. 62;
Iskusstvo Porty 2008, cat. 40.

45, 46. DISHES FOR SCENT BOTTLES
Turkey, Istanbul, first half 17th century
Rock crystal, gold, rubies, emeralds, paper
Carving, chasing, casting, painting
Diam. 13.5 cm
From the Main Collection of the Armory
Inv. nos. MV-36, MV-37

SOURCES: Opis' Oruzheinoi palaty 1835, no.
2378; Opis' Oruzheinoi palaty 1884–1893, ch.
2, kn. 1, nos. 522, 523, 524.

LITERATURE: Iskusstvo Porty 2008, cat. 46.

47. SCENT BOTTLE
Turkey, first half 17th century
Rock crystal, gold, rubies, emeralds
Carving, encrustation
H. 15 cm
From the Main Collection of the Armory
Inv. no. DK-270

SOURCES: Opis' Oruzheinoi palaty 1835, no.
2378; Opis' Oruzheinoi palaty 1884–1893, ch.
2, kn. 3, no. 2577.

LITERATURE: Vishnevskaya 1996, vol. 2, p.
213; Gifts to the Tsars 2001, no. 35; "Vo
utverzhdenie druzhby . . ." 2005, no. 60;
Iskusstvo Porty 2008, cat. 44.

48. WRITING SET
Turkey, 1660s–1670s
Gold, silver, lazurite, diamonds, rubies, pearls
Carving, chasing, enamel
Overall L. 27 cm; H. 7 cm
From the Main Collection of the Armory
Inv. no. MV-41

SOURCES: Opis' Oruzheinoi palaty 1835,
no. 277; Drevnosti 1853, vol. 5, p. 69; Opis'
Oruzheinoi palaty 1884–1893, ch. 2, kn. 3,
no. 2589.

LITERATURE: Putevoditel' 1960, ill. 16;
Vishnevskaya 1996, vol. 2, cat. 187; Gifts to
the Tsars 2001, cat. 36; Iskusstvo Porty 2008,
cat. 49.

49. POCKET WATCH WITH CALENDAR
Mechanism and face: Geneva, mid-17th
century; case: Istanbul, mid-17th century
Metal, gold, silver, diamonds, enamel
Chasing, carving, casting
H. 7 cm; W. 5 cm
From the Main Collection of the Armory
Inv. no. MV-4089

SOURCES: Opis' Oruzheinoi palaty 1884–
1893, ch. 1, no. 509.

LITERATURE: Putevoditel' 1960, p. 16;
Sokrovishcha Irana i Turtsii 1979, no. 163, ill.
on p. 60; Vishnevskaya 1996, p. 224, ill. 185,
186; Treasures 1997, cat. 13; Gifts to the Tsars
2001, cat. 37; "Vo utverzhdenie druzhby . . ."
2005, cat. 63; Iskusstvo Porty 2008, cat. 52.

50, 51. CUFFS FOR A HORSE
Russia, Moscow Kremlin workshops,
17th century
Silver
Chasing, gilding
H. each 8.5 cm
From the Main Collection of the Armory
Inv. nos. K-686, K-687

SOURCES: Opis' koniushennym veshcham
1706, ll. 217–19ob; Opis' Oruzheinoi palaty
1884–1893, ch. 6, kn. 5, no. 8810.

LITERATURE: The Arsenal 2007, pp. 33–34.

52. ORNAMENTAL HORSE CHAIN
Russia, Moscow Kremlin workshops,
17th century
Silver
Chasing, gilding, casting, carving
L. approximately 360 cm
From the Main Collection of the Armory
Inv. no. K-107/17

SOURCES: Opis' koniushennym veshcham
1706, "chains," l. 227ob, 231; Opis'
Oruzheinoi palaty 1884–1893, no. 9062.

LITERATURE: Treasures 1996, pp. 232–33;
The Arsenal 2007, pp. 21–22.

53. TASSEL
Russia, Moscow Kremlin workshops,
17th century
Silver, braid, pearls, gold threads
Weaving, chasing, carving, gilding, braiding
L. 75 cm
From the Main Collection of the Armory
Inv. no. K-677

SOURCES: Opis' koniushennym veshcham
1706, l. 128 ob; Opis' Oruzheinoi palaty
1884–1893, ch. 6, kn. 5, no. 8997.

LITERATURE: Orel i lev 2001, cat. 204;
Der Kreml 2004, cat. 152.

54. PAIR OF STIRRUPS
Russia, Moscow Kremlin workshops,
17th century
Silver, iron, braid
Forging, carving, flat chasing
H. each 15 cm
From the Main Collection of the Armory
Inv. no. K-1091/1–2

SOURCES: Opis' koniushennym veshcham
1706, sedla, no. 29, l. 150; Opis' Oruzheinoi
palaty 1884–1893, ch. 6, kn. 5, no. 8507.

LITERATURE: Splendeur 1993; The Arsenal
2007, pp. 17–18.

55. SADDLE
Russia, Moscow Kremlin workshops,
first half 17th century
Gold, silver, rubies, emeralds, nephrite, wood,
leather, velvet, braid, gilded threads
Gilding, chasing, carving, encrustation,
embroidery, weaving
L. 50 cm; H. of front pommel 33 cm
From the Main Collection of the Armory
Inv. no. K-1090

SOURCES: Opis' koniushennym veshcham
1706, sedla, no. 29, l. 149ob; Opis' Oruzheinoi
palaty 1884–1893, ch. 6, kn. 5, no. 8507.

LITERATURE: Splendeur 1993; The Arsenal
2007, pp. 15–16.

56. SABER AND SCABBARD OF
THE GRAND ATTIRE WITH BELT
Russia, Moscow Armory, first half 17th century;
blade: Turkey, first third 17th century
Gold, silver, steel, wood, braid, rubies,
emeralds

Forging, carving, flat chasing, enamel,
encrustation, damascening
Overall L. 105.5 cm; L. of blade 92 cm;
L. of sheath 95 cm
From the Main Collection of the Armory
Inv. no. OR-137/1–3

SOURCES: Perepisnaia kniga Oruzheinoi
kazne 1686/1687, l. 35; Opis' Oruzheinoi
palaty 1884–1893, ch. 4, kn. 3, no. 5903.

LITERATURE: Arsenal of the Russian Tsars
1998, cat. 4; Gosudareva Oruzheinaia palata
2002, no. 36; The Arsenal 2007, pp. 9–10.

57. PAIR OF ARMGUARDS
Russia, Moscow Armory, first half 17th
century; master: Nikita Davydov
Watered steel, braid
Forging, damascening
L. 35 cm; Weight 1466 g
From the Main Collection of the Armory
Inv. no. OR-4062

SOURCES: Opis' Oruzheinoi palaty 1884–
1893, ch. 3, kn. 2, no. 4653.

LITERATURE: Orel i lev 2001, no. 197;
Gosudareva Oruzheinaia palata 2002, cat. 29;
Tsar' Aleksei Mikhailovich 2005, no. 120.

58, 59. PAIR OF AMBASSADORIAL AXES
Turkey, early 17th century
Steel, gold, silver, wood
Forging, chasing, flat chasing, damascening,
gilding
L. 106.5 cm, 104.5 cm
From the Main Collection of the Armory
Inv. nos. OR-2234, OR-2235

SOURCES: Perechnevaia rospis' 1647, f. 396,
d. 3593; Perepisnaia kniga Oruzheinoi kazne
1686/1687, l. 133ob.; Opis' Oruzheinoi palaty
1884–1893, ch. 5, kn. 4, nos. 5271, 5272.

LITERATURE: Gosudareva Oruzheinaia palata
2002, cat. 63, pp. 210–11, 357; Czars 2002, p.
109, ill. on p. 102; The Arsenal 2007, pp. 23–24.

60. QUIVER AND BOW CASE
Russia, Moscow, 17th century
Leather, velvet, silver, silver and gold threads
Embroidery, carving, niello
L. of bow case 75 cm; L. of quiver 44.5 cm
From the Main Collection of the Armory
Inv. no. OR-148

SOURCES: Opis' Oruzheinoi palaty 1884–
1893, ch. 4, kn. 3, no. 6348.

LITERATURE: Chevaux 2002, cat. 112.

61. STIKHARION (SURPLICE) YOKE
Russia, mid-17th century; silk (altabas):
Turkey, 17th century; embroidery: Russia,
mid-17th century
Silk, canvas, gold, silver, precious gems, pearls
Embroidery, weaving, enamel, chasing
H. 46 cm; W. 38 cm
Accessioned from the Patriarchal Sacristy
in 1920
Inv. no. TK-41

SOURCES: Opis' Oruzheinoi palaty 1914–
1930, d. 13, l. 57ob, no. 12282.

LITERATURE: Mir iskusstva 1904, no. 10,
p. 216; Vishnevskaia 1995, p. 156; Iskusstvo
Porty 2008, cat. 68.

62. SAKKOS
Embroidery: Moscow, after 1658; satin body:
Turkey, late 16th–early 17th century; satin
front panel: Istanbul, 1670s
Gilded satin, velvet, taffeta, gold and silver
spun thread, braid, silver
Weaving, embroidery
L. 135 cm
From the Patriarchal Sacristy
Inv. no. TK-2208

SOURCES: Viktorov 1875, pp. 8, 18; Savva
1883, p. 22, no. 17; Opis' Oruzheinoi palaty
1914–1930, d. 13, no. 12034.

LITERATURE: Klein 1925, pp. 49–50, ill.
35; Levinson-Nechaeva 1954, p. 332;
Sokrovishcha Irana i Turtsii 1979, pp. 8, 51,
no. 136; Trezori 1985, p. 58; Schätze 1987,
cat. 17; Vishnevskaia 1996, p. 236, ills. 198,
199; Vishnevskaia 2007, cat. 20.

63. TABERNACLE
Russia (plaques), Moscow (tabernacle), first
quarter 18th century
Gold, silver, precious gems, stones, river pearls
Chasing, casting, enamel, niello, carving
H. 36 cm; W. 14 cm
From the Annunciation Cathedral of the
Moscow Kremlin
Inv. no. MR-3390/1–10

SOURCES: Opis' Blagoveshchenskogo sobora
1701–1703 gg., l. 89; Opisi Blagoveshchenskogo
sobora 1817, l. 116ob; 1854, l. 137ob; 1916 gg.,
ll. 91–93ob; Opis' Oruzheinoi palaty 1914–
1930, d. 12, l. 181ob, no. 11059.

LITERATURE: Shakurova 1987, pp. 23–24,
ills. 56–59; Zoloto Kremlia 1989, cat. 59;
Treasures 1995, p. 150; Tsaarien 1996, cat. 32;
Tsarskii khram 2003, cat. 72, pp. 219–23.

64. PLAQUE (PANAGIA)
Turkey, Istanbul, second half 17th century
Gold, emeralds, diamonds, rubies
Casting, enamel
L. 11 cm; W. 8 cm
From the Main Collection of the Armory
Inv. no. MV-399

SOURCES: Opis' Oruzheinoi palaty 1884–
1893, ch. 1, no. 439.

LITERATURE: Sokrovishcha Irana i Turtsii
1979, no. 176; Iskusstvo Porty 2008, cat. 63.

65. PECTORAL ICON (PANAGIA)
Turkey, Istanbul, first half 17th century
Silver, gold, precious gems
Chasing, carving, enamel
H. 15 cm; W. 8 cm
Acquired in 1926
Inv. no. MV-580
Published here for the first time.

DYNASTIC RULERS

Russia, Iran, and Turkey in the Sixteenth and Seventeenth Centuries

GRAND PRINCES OF MOSCOW

Rurik Dynasty

Ivan Vasilevich III (Ivan the Great)	1462–1505
Vasily Ivanovich III	1505–1533
Ivan Vasilevich IV (Ivan the Terrible)	1533–1547

TSARS OF RUSSIA

Rurik Dynasty

Ivan Vasilevich IV (Ivan the Terrible)	1547–1584
Fedor Ivanovich I	1584–1598

Time of Troubles

Borus Godunov	1598–1605
"False" Dmitry I	1605–1606
Vasily Shuisky IV	1606–1610

Interregnum

Romanov Dynasty

Mikhail Fedorovich I	1613–1645
Alexei Mikhailovich I	1645–1676
Fedor Alexevich III	1676–1682
Ivan Alexevich V	1682–1689
Petr I Alexevich (Peter the Great)	1682–1725

SHAHS OF SAFAVID IRAN

Isma`il I	1501–1524
Tahmasp	1524–1576
Isma`il II	1576–1578
Muhammad Khudabandeh	1578–1588
Abbas I	1588–1629
Safi I	1629–1642
Abbas II	1642–1666
Sulayman I (Safi II)	1666–1694
Husayn I	1694–1722

SULTANS OF OTTOMAN TURKEY

Bayezid II	1481–1512
Selim I	1512–1520
Süleyman I	1520–1566
Selim II	1566–1574
Murad III	1574–1595
Mehmed III	1595–1603
Ahmed I	1603–1617
Mustafa I	1617–1618; 1622–1623
Osman II	1618–1622
Murad IV	1623–1640
Ibrahim	1640–1648
Mehmed IV	1648–1687
Süleyman II	1687–1691
Ahmed II	1691–1695
Mustafa II	1695–1703

EASTERN TREASURES
OF THE RUSSIAN TSARS

1. Uspenskii 1912, p. 216.

2. Kniga tovaram persidskim 1904,
   pp. 1413–78.

3. Karpini 1957, p. 79.

4. Kramarovskii 1996, pp. 55–57.

5. For example, an animal facing right is
   depicted in a round double frame on
   the back of a *pul* from the reign of Khan
   Abdullah (Fedorov-Davydov 2003,
   p. 192, tab. 16, no. 223). Another appears
   on a Juchid *pul* (Fren 1832, p. 37,
   tab. 10, no. 338).

6. Kontarini 1835, p. 63.

7. Svanidze 1978, p. 18.

8. Kotoshikhin 1906, p. 71.

9. Kurts 1915, p. 146.

10. Kurts 1914, p. 155.

11. Kotoshikhin 1906, p. 7.

12. Chistiakov 1958, p. 124.

13. Sobranie Gosudarstvennykh gramot
    1828, ch. 4, no. 56.

14. Kakash i Tektander 1890, p. 7.

15. Khuan Persidskii, don 1899, pp. 1–19.

16. Solov'ev 1896, vol. 4, p. 240.

17. Kologrivov 1911, pp. 124–32.

18. Arkhiv drevnikh aktov 1991, vol. 1,
    p. 305.

19. Lebedev 1901, vol. 2, p. 343.

20. Floria 2004, pp. 248–87.

21. Posol'skie dela 1631–1632, ll. 92ob–99.

22. Kologrivov 1906, p. 12.

23. Ibid., p. 21.

24. Levykin 1997, p. 63.

25. Meier 1976, p. 10.

26. Cited in Novichev 1960, vol. 14, p. 31.

27. Vishnevskaya 1984, pp. 83–102.

28. Kologrivov 1906, p. 5.

RUSSIAN-IRANIAN RELATIONS

1. P. P. Bushev, *Istoriia posol'stv i diplomaticheskikh
   otnoshenii russkogo iranskogo gosudarstv
   v 1586–1612 gg.* (Moscow, 1976), 36, 39.

2. An exception is the Russian envoy who
   visited Iran in 1629, shortly after the
   accession of Shah Safi. He was accompanied
   by "seventeen falcons, a few furs, a gold-
   enameled goblet, fish teeth and other
   objects." See Muhammad Masum b. Khajigi
   Isfahani, *Khulasat al-siyar. Tarikh-i ruzgar-i
   Shah Safi Safavi* (Tehran, 1368/1989), 98.

3. *Gifts to the Tsars* 2001, 178.

4. For this, see Bushev, *Istoriia posol'stv . . .
   v 1586–1612 gg.* Also see P. P. Bushev,
   *Istoriia posol'stv i diplomaticheskikh
   otnoshenii russkogo iranskogo gosudarstv v
   1613–1621 gg.* (Moscow, 1987), and Rudi
   Matthee, "Anti-Ottoman Concerns and
   Caucasian Interests: Diplomatic Relations
   between Iran and Russia 1587–1629," in
   Michel Mazzaoui, ed., *Safavid Iran and her
   neighbors* (Salt Lake City, 2003), 101–28.

5. P. P. Bushev, "Puteshestvie iranskogo
   posol'stva Mokhammeda Khosein Khan-
   Beka v Moskvu v 1690–1692 vv.," *Strany
   i Narody Vostoka* 18 (1976): 135. For
   the difference between *veliki* ("heavy")
   and *legki* ("light") missions and those
   performed by messengers (*gontsi*), see
   M. Iu. Iuldasev, *K istorii torgovykh i
   posol'skikh zviazei srednei Azii s Rossiei v
   XVI–XVII vv.* (Tashkent, 1964), 23–24.

6. Nationaal Archief (Dutch National
   Archives), The Hague, VOC 1162,
   Verburgh, Gamron to Heren XVII, 4 May
   1647, fol. 181; E. S. Zevakin, "Konflikt
   Rossii s Persiei v seredine XVII stoletiia,"
   Azerbaidzhan v nachale XVIII veka 8/
   iv (Baku, 1929), 24; ibid.; and Wolfgang
   Sartor, "Die Wolga als internationaler
   Handelsweg für persische Rohseide im
   17. und 18. Jahrhundert," Ph.D. diss. Free
   University (Berlin, 1993), 82, fn. 40.

7. Muhammad Yusuf Valah Qazvini
   Isfahani, *Iran dar zaman-i Shah Safi va
   Shah `Abbas-i divvum (1038–1071 h.q.),*
   ed. Muhammad Riza Nasiri (Tehran,
   1380/2001), 509–10; Abu'l Hasan
   Qazvini, *Fava'id-i Safaviyah*, ed. Maryam
   Mir Ahmadi (Tehran, 1367/1988), 67.

8. Nationaal Archief, VOC 1203, Sarcerius,
   Gamron to Batavia, 16 May 1654, fol.
   815; E. Zevakin, "Konflikt Rossii s Perseie
   v seredine XVII stoletiia," *Azerbaidzhian
   v nachale XVIII veka* 8:4 (1929): 27;

9. Valah Qazvini Isfahani, *Iran dar zaman-i
   Shah Safi*, 530.

10. Zevakin, "Konflikt Rossii s Perseie," 29;
    Bushev, *Istoriia posol'stv . . . v 1613–1621*,
    178.

11. Jean Chardin, *Voyages du chevalier
    Chardin, en Perse, et autres lieux de l'Orient,*
    ed. by L. Langlès, 10 vols. and map (Paris,
    1810–11), 10:112ff. Chardin claims the
    embassy consisted of eight hundred people.
    In a letter from Isfahan written in early
    1665, in which he presumably refers to
    the same embassy, the Frenchman Daulier
    Deslandes mentions mechanical organs
    given to the shah by the Muscovites. See
    Anne Kroell, ed., *Nouvelles d'Ispahan
    1665–1695* (Paris, 1979), 18.

12. Chardin, *Voyages*, 10:113.

13. Vali Qazvini Isfahani, *Kuld-i barin*, 114.

14. Pietro della Valle, *Viaggi di Pietro della
    Valle il pellegrino*, ed. G. Gancia (Brighton,
    1843), 1:832, 2:41; and in general,
    Matthee, "Anti-Ottoman Concerns."

15. Nationaal Archief, VOC 1245, Van
    Wijck, Gamron to Heren XVII, 9 January
    1665, fols. 365v–66.

16. Nationaal Archief, VOC 1245, Van Wijck,
    Gamron to Heren XVII, 4 April 1665, fol.
    514v; Jean de Thevenot, "Relation d'un
    voyage fait au Levant," vol. 2, *Suite du
    voyage de Levant* (Paris, 1674), 202–204.

17. Chardin, *Voyages*, 10:114. Whether or
    not the Russians encouraged the Cossack
    raids, their incursions did intensify
    around the time of Shah Sulayman's
    succession. The Cossacks wreaked havoc
    on the Caspian littoral, where they
    destroyed the town of Farahabad, built
    by Shah Abbas I as a winter resort, and
    captured and killed hundreds of people.

18. Vahan Baibourtian, *International Trade
    and the Armenian Merchants in the
    Seventeenth Century* (New Delhi, 2004),
    152–53; Giampiero Bellingeri, "Sugli
    Sceriman rimasti a Giulfa: devozione
    agli sultimi Safavidi?" in Boghos Levon
    Zekiyan and Aldo Ferrari, eds., *Gli Armeni
    e Venezia. Dagli Scermina a Mechitar: il
    momento culminante di ana consuetifine
    millenaria* (Venice, 2004), 109.

19. E. S. Zevakin, "Persidskii vopros v
    russko-evropeiskikh otnosheniiakh XVII
    v." *Istorichekie Zapiski* 8 (1940), 129–62
    (143–44).

EXHIBITION CATALOGUE

1. Georgievskii 1927, pl. 14, figs. 1, 2.

2. Opis' Oruzheinoi palaty 1808, vol. 2, ch. 2, otd. 4, no. 2718, l. 224.

3. Opis' Oruzheinoi palaty 1835; Opis' Oruzheinoi palaty 1884–1893.

4. Martin 1899, p. 15.

5. Timur and the Princely Vision 1989, cat. 116.

6. Opis' Oruzheinoi palaty 1884–1893, ch. 2, kn. 3, no. 3742, p. 220.

7. The basic elements of this ornament (a stylized image of "Chinese clouds") are believed to be of Chinese origin and were widely disseminated throughout the Near and Middle East during the Timurid period.

8. "The price of the shield as appraised by the gunsmith Afanas'ii Viatkin and others is 1000 rubles" (Perepisnaia kniga Oruzheinoi kazne 1686/1687, l. 186, no. 1). "To judge by the hole on the top we must conclude that the shield once had a knob that is no longer extant" (Opis' Oruzheinoi palaty 1808, p. 1330, no. 6625).

9. Petrey 1997, p. 303.

10. Massa 1997, pp. 68, 69.

11. Here and elsewhere the translations of Arabic inscriptions are taken from the text of the Armory inventory of 1884–1893.

12. Opis' Oruzheinoi palaty 1884–1893, ch. 3, kn. 2, 4404, 4405, 4406.

13. Alexander 1992, p. 66.

14. Opis' koniushennym veshcham 1706, l. 306ob.

15. Similar fringe adorned the covering with lions. It was probably removed at the time of its exhibition at the State Hermitage in the 1930s and now is kept separately.

16. Umeni 1966, p. 463; Pirverdian 1971, p. 4.

17. Ibid.

18. Reath-Sachs 1937, p. 121, example 79; Survey of Persian Art 1964, vol. 6, pp. 2070–138; vol. 12, p. 1081.

19. An Illustrated Souvenir 1931, N 376B.

20. Oreshnikov 1911, pp. 483–86.

21. Rospis' pokhodnoi kazny 1654–1655, l. 88.

22. Prikhodnaia kniga 1616–1617, l. 34.

23. Vishnevskaya 1996, vol. 2, pp. 199–207.

24. On the gifts brought by the ambassador Muhammad Selim Beg in 1629, see Prikhodnaia kniga 1628–1629, ll. 51–59.

25. Denisova 1954, p. 278; Sokrovishcha Irana i Turtsii 1979, no. 25; Vishnevskaya 1987; Mironova 1996, no. 151.

26. Posol'skaia kniga 1640–1643.

27. Ibid, l. 189ob–193ob.

28. Ibid., l. 232.

29. Opis' koniushennym veshcham 1706, ll. 3–3ob.

30. Perepisnaia kniga Oruzheinoi kazne 1686/1687, l. 509, no. 1. "Steel iushman from the Tsar's old court, incised with gold with words and Arabic grasses on the plates."

31. Rospis' pokhodnoi kazny 1654–1655, no. 4; Perepisnaia kniga Oruzheinoi kazne 1686/1687, l. 461, no. 2.

32. The term rumi comes from the Turkish for "Greek." This type of ornament was common in the territories of Asia Minor by the Byzantine and Seljuq periods.

33. Atil 1987, no. 208.

34. Zemnoe iskusstvo 2000, no. 302.

35. Atil 1987, p. 125.

36. Opis' 1663–1666, l. 200.

37. Alexander 1992, p. 120, no. 67.

38. Kologrivov 1911, pp. 148, 151.

39. The saddle in question is the first listed in the section "new archaks made in the Stable Treasury." Judging by this information, the saddle can be dated to the 1680s and before 1686/1687, the year on which the 1706 inventory was based. The archak (saddle with a cushion on the seat) listed as number ninety-eight was covered in gold brocade (altabas) and had a gold frame with gems and painted enamel. It is currently on exhibit in the halls of the Armory.

40. In the mid-twentieth century M. M. Denisova confirmed that the bridle had been transferred from the Foreign Office in 1623 and was now housed in the Kremlin Museums. Subsequent comparisons of the items in the museum with the 1706 inventory of the Stable Treasury made it possible to verify that the chest straps as well as the bridle had survived.

41. Royal Swedish Armory, Stockholm, inv. nos. 9044, 31201. The set was a gift to the king of Sweden, Gustav II Adolf, on the occasion of his marriage to Princess Maria Eleonora of Brandenburg in 1626 (Hellner 1990, no. 28, pp. 90–91, fig. 69).

42. Atasoy 2002, pp. 38–39, nos. 33–34; p. 22, no. 99; p. 106, no. 132; p. 113, no. 145; p. 136, no. 181; p. 152, no. 208.

43. Atil 1987, p. 119.

44. Posol'skie dela 1631–1632, ll. 289, 372.

45. Vishnevskaya 1996, p. 225, ill. 187.

46. Drevnosti 1853, p. 69.

47. Atasoy 2002, p. 136, no. 181; p. 74, no. 72.

48. Sokrovishcha Irana i Turtskii 1979, no. 163, ill. on p. 60; Vishnevskaya 1996, p. 224, ills. 185–86.

49. Tanner 1891, p. 45.

50. Opis' kazny Borisa Godunova 1588, l. 114.

51. Opis' sedel'noi kazny 1610.

52. Opis' koniushennym veshcham 1706, l. 128ob.

53. The 1884–1893 inventory of the Armory includes a translation of the Arabic inscription "I firmly establish," together with the date 1041 by the Muslim calendar. Unfortunately, the almost complete loss of the inscription makes it impossible to confirm the transcription's accuracy.

54. Levinson-Nechaeva 1954, p. 332.

55. Vishnevskaya 1984.

56. Viktorov 1875, p. 8.

57. Ibid., p. 18.

58. Posol'skaia kniga 1627, l. 112.

59. Posol'skaia kniga 1630, ll. 4, 6, 256–57.

60. Posol'skaia kniga 1633, l. 265.

61. Posol'skaia kniga 1634–36, ll. 36, 40, 505.

62. Kologrivov 1911, p. 143. They were valued at 1,000 and 156 rubles, respectively.

BIBLIOGRAPHY

LIST OF ABBREVIATIONS

GIM   State Historical Museum

GE   State Hermitage

Muzei Moskovskogo Kremlin
   "Moscow Kremlin" State Museum
   Reserve of History and Culture

ORGPF   Muzeev Moskovskogo Kremlia
   Division of Manuscripts, Prints
   and Graphic Funds of the
   Moscow Kremlin Museums

RGADA   Russian State Archive of Ancient
   Documents

RGIA   Russian State Historical Archive

ARCHIVAL AND PRIMARY SOURCES

Dela Persidskogo dvora 1618–1624
RGADA, Dela Persidskogo dvora, no. 6, 1618–1624.

Kakash i Tektander 1890
Kakash i Tektander. *Puteshestvie v Persiiu cherez Moskoviiu v 1602–1603 godakh.* Trans. Stankevich. Moscow, 1890.

Karpini 1957
Karpini, Plano. *Istoriia mongolov.* Moscow, 1957.

Khuan Persidskii, don 1899
Khuan Persidskii, don. *Puteshestvie persidskogo posol'stva cherez Rossiiu, ot Astrakhani do Arkhangel'ska, v 1599–1500 gg. Iz rasskazov don Khuana Persidskogo.* Trans. Sokolov. Moscow, 1899, pp. 1–19.

Kniga tovaram persidskim 1904
Kniga perepisnaia tovaram persidskim. Russkaia istoricheskaia biblioteka, vol. 23. St. Petersburg, 1904.

Kontarini 1835
Puteshestvie Amvrosimo Kontarini posla svetleishei Venetsianskoi respubliki k znamenitomu persidskomu gosudariiu Uzun-Gassanu, sovershennoe v 1473g. Biblioteka inostrannykh pisatelei o Rossii, vol. 1. St. Petersburg, 1835.

Kopii s ukazov 1721–1731
Kopii s ukazov i s vypisok o raskhode Koniuzhennoi kazny per'ev, sanei, uzd, karet, chaldarov, cheprakov i prochikh koniushennykh uborov s 1721 po 1731 god. RGADA, f. 396, op. 2, ch. 3 d. 1250.

Kotoshikhin 1906
Kotoshikhin, G. O. *Rossiia v tsarstvovanie Alekseiia Mikhailovicha.* St. Petersburg, 1906.

Massa 1997
Massa, I. *Kratkoe izvestie o Moskovii. (O nachale voin i smut v Moskovii).* Moscow, 1997.

Opis' 1663–1666
Opis' tsarskoi kazny na Kazennom dvore 1663–1666 gg. RGADA, f. 396, op. 2, ch. 1, d. 8.

Opis' 1676
Opis' tsarskoi kazny na Kazennom dvore 1676 g. RGADA, f. 396, op. 2, ch. 1, d. 9.

Opis' Blagoveshchenskogo sobora 1701–1703
Kopii opisnykh bumag Blagoveshchenskogo sobora 1701–1703 (1721). RGADA, f. 196, op. 1, d. 105.

Opis' Blagoveshchenskogo sobora 1817
Opis' tserkovnogo imushchestva Blagoveshchenskogo sobora za 1817 g. ORGPF Muzeev Moskovskogo Kremlia, f. 3, d. 105.

Opis' Blagoveshchenskogo sobora 1854
Opis' tserkovnogo imushchestva Blagoveshchenskogo sobora za 1854 g. ORGPF Muzeev Moskovskogo Kremlia, f. 3, d. 115.

Opis' Blagoveshchenskogo sobora 1916
Opis' tserkovnogo imushchestva Blagoveshchenskogo sobora za 1916 g. ORGPF Muzeev Moskovskogo Kremlia, f. 3, d. 122.

Opis' kazny Borisa Godunova 1588
Kniga perepisnaia pozhitkam Borisa Fedorovicha 1588 g. RGADA, f. 396, op. 2, ch. 1, d. 2.

Opis' keleinoi kazny 1876
Opis' keleinoi kazny pariarkha Filareta Nikiticha. Russkaia istoricheskaia biblioteka, vol. 3. St. Petersburg, 1863.

Opis' koniushennym veshcham 1706
Opis' raznym koniushennym veshcham i kazne 1706 g. RGADA, f. 296, op. 2, ch. 2, d. 1022.

Opis' Novodevich'ego monastyria 1861
Glavnaia opis' tserkovnogo imushchestva moskovskogo Novodevich'ego monastyria sostavlennaia v 1808 g. GIM, d. 103971.

Opis' Oruzheinoi palaty 1808
Opis' veshcham Moskovskoi Oruzheinoi palaty po Vysochaishemu poveleniiu sostavlennaia v 1808 g. RGIA, f. 468, op. 1, 2, d. 400.

Opis' Oruzheinoi palaty 1808/2
Opis' veshcham Moskovskoi Oruzheinoi palaty 1808 g. RGADA, f. 386, op. 2, d. 124a.

Opis' Oruzheinoi palaty 1835
Opis' veshcham Moskovskoi Oruzheinoi palaty 1835 g. ORGPF Muzeev Moskovskogo Kremlia, f. 1, op. 2, d. 2.

Opis' Oruzheinoi palaty 1884–1893
Opis' Oruzheinoi palaty, vols. 1–7. Moscow, 1884–1893.

Opis' Oruzheinoi palaty 1914–1930
Opis' Oruzheinoi palaty 1914–1930 g. ORGPF Muzeev Moskovskogo Kremlia, f. 1, op. 3, d. 11–18.

Opis' oruzhiia 1810
Opis' Imperatorskoi Riustkamera 1810 g. RGADA, f. 396, op. 2, ch. 3, d. 1285.

Opis' sedel'noi kazny 1610
Opis' . . . gosudarevoi sedel'noi kazny [tsaria Vasiliia Shuiskogo] 118 (1610) g. RGADA, f. 396, op. 1, ch. 23, d. 36208.

Opis' tsarskoi kazny 1634
Opis' tsarskoi kazny na Kazennom dvore 1634 g. RGADA, f. 396, op. 2, ch. 1, d. 3.

Opis' tsarskoi kazny 1640
Opis' tsarskoi kazny na Kazennom dvore, sostavlennaia Samoilom Kirkintsym i d'iakom Timofeem Golosovym v 1640 g. RGADA, f. 396, op. 2, ch. 1, d. 4.

Opis' tsaria Ivana Vasil'evicha 1850
"Opis' domashnemu imushchestvu tsaria Ivana Vasil'evicha," in *Vremennik OIDR,* vol. 7. Moscow, 1850.

Perepisnaia kniga Oruzheinoi kazne 1686/1687
Perepisnaia kniga Oruzheinoi i vsiakoi tsarskoi kazne i krasok, chto v Oruzheinom palate, v Bol'shoi kazne, i v prochikh palatakh . . . 195 (1686/1687) g. RGADA, f. 396, op. 2, ch. 2, d. 936.

Perechnevaia rospis' 1647
Perechnevaia rospis' Oruzheinoi kazny tsaria Alekseia Mikhailovicha 1647 g. RGADA, f. 396, d. 3593.

Petrey 1997
Petrey, Petr, "Istoriia o velikom kniazhestve Moskovskom," in *O nachale voin i smut v Moskovii.* Moscow, 1997.

Posol'skaia kniga 1627, 1630, 1633, 1634–1636, 1640–1643, 1664–1665
Kniga . . . soderzhashchaia priezd k gosudariu ot shakha Sefiia s gramotoiu i podarkami posla Asan-beka i kupchiny Agi Magmeteva, zapiski o bytii ikh u gosudaria na audientsii, o sluchivsheisia poslu potom skoroi smerti i o priniatii po nem vsekh posol'skikh del bratom ego Saavakhan-bekom. RGADA.

Posol'skie dela 1631–1632
Vozvratnyi priezd Sovina i Alfimova . . . Otpravalenie na Don voevod kn. I. Boriatinskogo i G. Orlova, a v pristavakh K. Navalkina dlia vstrechi i preprovozhdeniia v Moskvu posla Mutoforana Akhmet Agi, priezd ego v Moskvu i preiekhavshikh s nim arkhimandritov tsar'gradskikh . . . RGADA, f. 89, op. 1, ch. 2, d. 2.

Prikhodnaia kniga 1616–1617
Prikhodnaia kniga 1616–1617. RGADA, f. 386, op. 2, ch. 1, d. 145.

Rospis' pokhodnoi kazny 1654–1655
[Rospis' pokhodnoi oruzheinoi kazny tsaria Alekseia Mikhailovicha, chto byla v Smolenskom pokhode 1654–1655 g.] RGADA, f. 396, d. 5835.

Rospis' Romanova 1887
Rospis' vsiakim veshcham, den'gam i zapasam, shto ostalos' po smerti boiarina Nikity Ivanovicha Romanova, vol. 3. Moscow, 1887.

Savva 1883
Savva, episkop Tverskoi. *Ukazatel' dlia obozreniia Moskovskoi Patriarshei (nyne Sinodal'noi) riznitsy i biblioteki.* Moscow, 1883.

Sobranie Gosudarstvennykh gramot 1828
Sobranie Gosudarstvennykh gramot i dogovorov, khraniashchikhsia v Gosudarstvennoi Kollegii inostrannykh del. Moscow, 1813–1894.

Tanner 1891
Tanner, B. *Opisanie puteshestviia pol'skogo posol'stva v Mosvky v 1678 godu.* Moscow, 1891.

SOURCES IN RUSSIAN

Arkhiv drevnikh aktov 1991
Tsentral'nyi gosudarstvennyi arkhiv drevnikh aktov SSSR. Putevoditel', vol. 1. Moscow 1991.

Chistiakov 1958
Chistiakov, V. P. "Novotorgovyi ustav 1667 g.," in *Arkheograficheskii ezhegodnik za 1957 g.* Moscow, 1958.

Denisova 1954
Denisova, M. M. "'Koniushennaia kazna.' Paradnoe konskoe ubranstvo XVI–XVII vekov," in *Gosudarstvennaia Oruzheinaia palata Moskovskogo Kremlia: Sbornik nauchnykh trudov po materialam Gos. Oruzheinoi palaty.* Moscow, 1954.

Drevnosti 1853
Drevnosti Rossiiskogo gosudarstva, vol. 5. Moscow, 1853.

Fedorov-Davydov 2003
Fedorov-Davydov, G. A. *Denezhnoe delo Zolotoi Ordy.* Moscow, 2003.

Floria 2004
Floria, B. N. "Foma Kantakuzin i ego rol' v razvitii russko-osmanskikh otnoshenii v 20-30-kh gg. XVII veka," in *Rossiia i khristianskii vostok. Sbornik statei,* vols. 2–3. Moscow, 2004.

Fren 1832
Fren, Kh. M. *Monety Ulusa Dzhuchieva ili Zolotoi Ordy.* St. Petersburg, 1832.

Georgievskii 1927
Georgievskii, V. T. *Pamiatniki starinnogo russkogo iskusstva Suzdal'skogo muzeia.* Moscow, 1927.

Gosudareva Oruzheinaia palata 1969
Gosudareva Oruzheinaia palata Moskovskogo Kremlia. Moscow, 1969.

Gosudareva Oruzheinaia palata 2002
Gosudareva Oruzheinaia palata [Al'bom]. St. Petersburg, 2002.

Imperatorskaia Riust-kamera 2004
Moskovskii Kreml'. Imperatorskaia Riust-kamera [Al'bom]. St. Petersburg, 2004.

Iskusstvo Porty 2008
Iskusstvo blistatel'noi Porty. Katalog vystavki. Moscow, 2008.

Kirillova 1964
Kirillova, L. P. "Koniushennaia kazna," in *Oruzheinaia palata.* Moscow, 1964.

Klein 1925
Klein, V. K. "Inozemnye tkani, bytovavshie v Rossii do XVIII veka i ikh terminologiia," *Sbornik Oruzheinoi palaty.* Moscow, 1925.

Kologrivov 1906
Kologrivov, S. N. *Zapisnye vznosnye knigi Bol'shomu gosudarevu nariadu.* St. Petersburg, 1906.

Kologrivov 1911
Kologrivov, S. N. "Materialy dlia istorii snoshenii Rossii s inostrannymi derzhavami v XVII veke," *Vestnik arkheologii i istorii,* vol. 2. St. Petersburg, 1911.

Kramarovskii 1996
Kramarovskii, M. G. "Vostok v moskovskoi filigrani kontsa XIV–pervoi poloviny XV v." in *Iskusstvo Vizantii i Drevnei Rusi. K 100-letiiu so dnia rozhdeniia A. N. Grabaria. Tezisy dokladov.* Moscow, 1996.

Kurts 1914
Kurts, B. G. *Sostoianie Rossii v 1650–55 godov po doneseniiam Rodesa.* Moscow, 1914.

Kurts 1915
Kurts, B. G. *Sochineniia Kil'burgera o russkoi torgovle v tsarstvovanie Alekseia Mikhailovicha.* Kiev, 1915.

Lebedev 1901
Lebedev, A. P. *Istoriia Greko-vostochnoi tserkvi pod vlast'iu turok,* vol. 2. Sergiev Posad, 1901.

Levinson-Nechaeva 1954
Levinson-Nechaeva, M. N. "Odezhda i tkani XVI–XVII vekov," in *Gosudarstvennaia Oruzheinaia palata Moskovskogo Kremlia.* Moscow, 1954.

Levykin 1997
Levykin, A. K. *Voinskie tseremonii i regalii russkikh tsarei.* Moscow, 1997.

Martynova 1984
Martynova, M. V. "Oklad ikony 'Bogomater' Mlekopitatel'nitsa' iz sobraniia muzeev Moskovskogo Kremlia," *Drevnerusskoe iskusstvo. XIV–XV vv.* Moscow, 1984.

Meier 1976
Meier, M. S. "Nekotorye tipologicheskie cherty osmanskogo feodalizma," in *Istoriia i filologiia Turtsii. Tezisy dokladov i soobshchenii Instituta vostokovedeniia Akademii nauk SSSR.* Moscow, 1976.

Melnikova 2004
Melnikova, O. B. "Komplekty sbrui XVII veka v Koniushennoi kazne Oruzheinoi palaty," in *Filimonovskie chteniia,* vol. 1. Moscow, 2004.

Mir iskusstva 1904
Mir iskusstva. St. Petersburg, 1898–1904.

Mironova 1996
Mironova, O. I. "Vostochnoe paradnoe konskoe ubranstvo," in *Sokrovishcha Oruzheinoi palaty. Posol'skie dary.* Moscow, 1996.

139

Mishukov 1954

Mishukov, F. Ia. Zolotaia nasechka i inkrustatsiia na drevnem vooruzhenii," in *Gosudarstvennaia Oruzheinaia palata Moskovskogo Kremlia: Sbornik nauchnykh trudov po materialam Gos. Oruzheinoi palaty.* Moscow, 1954.

Novichev 1960

Novichev, A. D. "Naselenie Osmanskoi imperii v XV–XVI vv.," in *Vestnik Leningradskogo universiteta*, vol. 14 (1960).

Orel i lev 2001

Orel i lev: Rossiia i Shvetsiia v XVII veke. Katalog vystavki. Moscow, 2001.

Oreshnikov 1911

Oreshnikov, A. V. "Pribavlenie tret'ei korony na dvuglavom orle," *Numizmaticheskii sbornik*, vol. 1. Moscow, 1911.

Oreshnikov 1928

Oreshnikov, A. V. "Persten' sv. Mitropolita Aleksiia," *Seminarium Kondakovianum.* Prague, 1928.

Oruzheinaia palata 1964

Oruzheinaia palata. Moscow, 1964.

Oruzheinaia palata 2006

Oruzheinaia palata Moskovskogo Kremlia. Moscow, 2006.

Pirverdian 1971

Pirverdian, N. A. *Srednevekovye persidskie khudozhestvennye tkani.* Leningrad, 1971.

Putevoditel' 1960

Putevoditel' po vystavke iranskogo i turetskogo iskusstva XVI–XVII vekov. Moscow, 1960.

Rossiiskie imperatory 2006

Rossiiskie imperatory i Oruzheinaia palata. Katalog vystavki. Moscow, 2006.

Shakurova 1987

Shakurova, E. V. "Russkie zolotye izdeliia XIV–XVII vekov," in *Russkoe zoloto XIV–nachala XX vekov iz fondov Gosudarstvennykh muzeev Moskovskogo Kremlia.* Moscow, 1987.

Svanidze 1978

Svanidze, M. Kh. Turetsko-iranskie otnosheniia v nachale XVII v. i Gruziia," in *Problemy istorii Turtsii. Sbornik statei.* Moscow, 1978.

Sokrovishcha Irana i Turtsii 1979

Sokrovishcha prikladnogo iskusstva Irana i Turtsii XVI–XVII vekov iz sobraniia Gosudarstvennykh muzeev Moskovskogo Kremlia: Katalog. Author of introductory article and compiler of catalogue, I. I. Vishnevskaia. Moscow 1979.

Solov'ev 1896

Solov'ev, S. M. *Istoriia Rossii s drevneishikh vremen*, vol. 4. St. Petersburg, 1896.

Tsarskii khram 2003

Tsarskii khram. Sviatyni Blagoveshchenskogo sobora v Kremle. Katalog vystavki. Moscow, 2003.

Tsar' Aleksei Mikhailovich 2005

Tsar' Aleksei Mikhailovich i Patriarkh Nikon. Katalog vystavki. Moscow, 2005.

Uspenskii 1912

Uspenskii, A. I. *Stolbtsy byvshego Arkhiva Oruzheinoi palaty*, vol. 1. Moscow, 1912.

Vera i vlast' 2007

Vera i vlast'. Epokha Ivana Groznogo. Katalog. Moscow, 2007.

Viktorov 1875

Viktorov, A. E. "Obozrenie starinnykh opisei Patriarshei riznitsy," *Vestnik Obshchestva drevnerusskogo iskusstva pri Moskovskom publichnom muzee*, vols. 6–10 (1875).

Viktorov 1877

Viktorov, A. E. *Opisanie zapisnykh knig i bumag starinnykh dvortsovykh prikazov v 1584–1725 gg.*, vol. 1. Moscow, 1877.

Vishnevskaya 1984

Vishnevskaya, I. I. "K voprosu ob atributsii tkani sakkosa mitropolita Dionisiia," in *Proizvedeniia russkogo i zarubezhnogo iskusstva XVI-nachala XVIII veka. Materialy i issledovaniia.* Moscow, 1984

Vishnevskaya 1987

Vishnevskaya, I. I. "Gruppa predmetov paradnogo konskogo ubranstva iranskoi raboty XVI–XVII vekov iz sobraniia Muzeev Kremlia," in *Muzei Kremlia. Materialy i issledovaniia. Novye atributsii.* Moscow, 1987.

Vishnevskaya 1996

Vishnevskaya, I. I. "Iuvelirnye izdeliia i torevtika Vostoka," in *Sokrovishcha Oruzheinoi palaty. Posol'skie dary.* Moscow, 1996.

Vishnevskaya 2007

Vishnevskaya, I. I. *Dragotsennye tkani.* Moscow, 2007.

"Vo utverzhdenie druzhby . . ." 2005

"Vo utverzhdenie druzhby . . ." Posol'skie dary russkim tsariam. Katalog vystavki. Moscow, 2005.

Yablonskaya 1996

Yablonskaya, E. A. "Paradnoe vooruzhenie," in *Sokrovishcha Oruzheinoi palaty. Posol'skie dary.* Moscow, 1996.

Zagorodnyaya 2005

Zagorodnyaya, I. A. "Istoriia tsarskoi kazny v zerkale vneshnei politiki Rossii XVII stoletiia," in *"Vo utverzhdenie druzhby . . ." Posol'skie dary russkim tsariam. Katalog vystavki.* Moscow, 2005.

Zemnoe iskusstvo 2000

Zemnoe iskusstvo–nebesnaia krasota. Edited by M. B. Piotrovsky. St. Petersburg, 2000.

Zolotaia orda 2005

Zolotaia Orda. Istoriia i kul'tura. St. Petersburg, 2005.

Zoloto Kremlia 1989

Zoloto Kremlia. Katalog vystavki. Munich, 1989.

SOURCES IN OTHER LANGUAGES

Alexander 1992

Alexander, David. *The Arts of War. Arms and Armour of the 7th to 19th Centuries. The Nasser D. Khalili Collection of Islamic Art*, vol. 21. New York, 1992.

Arsenal of the Russian Tsars 1998

Treasures of the Moscow Kremlin. Arsenal of the Russian Tsars. A Royal Armouries Exhibition. London, 1998.

The Arsenal 2007

The Arsenal of the Russian Tsars: Treasures of the Moscow Kremlin Museums. Abu Dhabi, 2007.

Atasoy 2002

Atasoy, Nurhan. *A Garden for the Sultan: Gardens and Flowers in the Ottoman Culture.* Aygaz, Turkey, 2002.

Atil 1987

Atil, Esin. *The Age of Sultan Süleyman the Magnificent.* Washington, D.C., 1987.

Die Ausstellung 1910

Die Ausstellung von Meisterwerken Muhammedanischer Kunst in München 1910. Munich, 1912.

Chevaux 2002

Chevaux et cavaliers arabes dans les arts d'Orient et d'Occident. Exposition présentée à l'Institut du monde arabe. Paris, 2002.

Czars 2002

Czars: 400 Years of Imperial Grandeur. Memphis, Tenn., 2002.

Gifts to the Tsars 2001

Gifts to the Tsars 1500–1700. Treasures of the Kremlin. Edited by Barry Shifman and Guy Walton. New York, 2001.

Hellner 1990

Hellner, Brynof. *Drottning Kristinas Rustkammare. Livrustkammaren.* Stockholm, 1990.

An Illustrated Souvenir 1931
An Illustrated Souvenir of the Exhibition of Persian Art. London, 1931.

Der Kreml 2004
Der Kreml: Gottesruhm und Zarenpracht. Munich, 2004.

Martin 1899
Martin, F. R. *Figurale Persische Stoffe.* Stockholm, 1899.

Reath-Sachs 1937
Reath, Nancy Andrews, and Eleanor B. Sachs. *Persian Textiles and Their Technique from the Sixth to the Eighteenth Centuries, including a system for general textile classification.* New Haven, Conn., 1937.

Remekmuvek 1989
Remekmuvek a cari kunstarbol. Parade es vadaszat a XVII szazadi oroszgban. Budapest, 1989.

Schätze 1987
Schätze der Museen des Moskauer Kreml. Berlin, 1987.

Schätze 1991
Schätze aus dem kreml: Peter der Grosse in Westeuropa. Munich, 1991.

Skatter fra Kreml 2001
Skatter fra Kreml. Utstilliungskatalog. Oslo, 2001.

Splendeur 1993
Splendeur equestre du Kremlin. Paris, 1993.

Survey of Persian Art 1964
A Survey of Persian Art from Prehistoric Times to the Present. Edited by Arthur Upham Pope and Phyllis Ackerman. Tokyo, 1964.

Tesoros 1990
Tesoros del Kremlin: Ceremonial de la gala en la Rusia del siglo XVII: Desfile de gala y caz a real. Moscow, 1990.

Timur and the Princely Vision 1989
Timur and the Princely Vision: Persian Art and Culture in the Fifteenth Century. Edited by Thomas W. Lentz and Glenn D. Lowry. Washington, D.C., 1989.

Treasures 1995
Treasures of the Czars from the State Museums of the Moscow Kremlin. London, 1995.

Treasures 1996
Treasures of the Tsar. Court Culture of Peter the Great from the Kremlin. Rotterdam, 1995–1996.

Treasures 1997
Sokrovishcha Kremla: khudozhestvennye chasy/Treasures of the Kremlin: Masterpieces of Horology. Geneva, 1997.

Trezori 1985
Trezori muzeja moskovskog Kremlja. Katalog izlozbe. Moscow, 1985.

Tsaarin 1996
Tsaarin ajan aareita. Punkaharju, Finland, 1996.

Umeni 1966
'Umeni' XIV.N5. Prague, 1966.

Vishnevskaya 1995
Vishnevskaya, I. I. "The Royal Court and the Orthodox Church in the Seventeenth Century," in *Treasures of the Czars from the State Museums of the Moscow Kremlin.* London, 1995.

Compiled by O. B. Melnikova

INDEX

CONCORDANCE

Numbers refer to catalogue entries

Bowl, 42, 44
Dish for scent bottle, 45, 46
Flask, 25
Horn, 16
Icon, 1
Panagia, 64, 65
Pocket watch, 49
Sakkos, 62
Scent bottle, 47
Seal ring [page 3]
Staff, 17
Tabernacle, 63
Tankard, 43
Textiles, 4, 9, 28, 30
Vestments, 2, 3, 61, 62
Writing set, 48

ARMS AND ARMOR
Ambassadorial ax, 58, 59
Armguard, 57
Broadsword, 12
Chain-mail shirt, 20
Dagger, 15, 23
Helmet, 8, 21
Mace, 14, 26
Saber, 6, 7, 13, 24, 56
Saadak, 36, 60
Shield, 5, 27

HORSE TRAPPINGS
Bridle, 18, 35, 37, 39
Caparison, 11, 22, 29, 31
Chain, 52
Chest strap, 36, 38, 40
Crupper, 41
Cuff, 50, 51
Saddle, 19, 32, 55
Saddle blanket, 10
Saddlecloth, 31
Stirrups, 33, 34, 54
Tassel, 53

CONTRIBUTORS

ARTHUR M. SACKLER GALLERY

Director: Julian Raby

Chief Curator: Massumeh Farhad

Head of Design and Production: Karen Sasaki

Editors: Nancy Eickel, Jane Lusaka

Catalogue Design: Marty Ittner

Translator: Wendy Salmond

Exhibition Graphics: Reid Hoffman

Image and Photo Services: John Tsantes

Exhibition Coordinator: Cheryl Sobas, Kelly Swain

MOSCOW KREMLIN MUSEUMS

Director General: Elena Yurievna Gagarina

Chief Curator: Olga Ivanovna Mironova

Assistant Director of Exhibitions: Zelfira Ismailovna Tregulova

Director of Science: Alexey Konstantinovich Levykin

Head of Arms and Armor Department: Olga Borisovna Melnikova

Head of Textiles Department: Inna Isidorovna Vishnevskaya

Head of International Department: Anastasia Nikitichna Parshina

Exhibition Conception

Alexey Konstantinovich Levykin

Inna Isidorovna Vishnevskaya

Olga Borisovna Melnikova

Elena Alexandrovna Yablonskaya

Exhibition Installation

Olga Borisovna Melnikova

Elena Alexandrovna Yablonskaya, *curator*

Nikolay Mikhailovich Maresev, *metalwork conservator*

Svetlana Alexandrovna Matyukhova, *textile conservator*

Conservation

Vladimir Arkadievich Vychuzhanin, *Head of Conservation Department*

Nikolay Mikhailovich Maresev, *metalwork conservator*

Mikhail Nikolaevich Kruzhalin, *metalwork conservator*

Mikhail Petrovich Anokhin, *metalwork conservator*

Tatiana Nikolaevna Vashchenko, *textile conservator*

Irina Mikhailovna Kachanova, *textile conservator*

Valentina Sergeevna Shabelnik, *textile conservator*

Svetlana Alexandrovna Matyukhova, *textile conservator*

Lyudmila Alexandrovna Barbinova, *textile conservator*

Photographers

Sergey Valentinovich Baranov

Viktor Nikolaevich Seregin

Valentin Yevgenievich Overchenko

Authors of Catalogue Entries

Irina Akimovna Bobrovnitskaya, 63

Natalia Viktorovna Bushueva, page 3, figure 2

Alexander Nikolaevich Chubinsky, 58, 59

Igor Alexandrovich Komarov, 20

Alexey Konstantinovich Levykin, 13, 24, 56

Marina Vasilievna Martynova, 1

Olga Borisovna Melnikova, 18, 19, 31–41, 50–55

Vasily Rudolfovich Novoselov, 6, 7, 12, 57

Inna Isidorovna Vishnevskaya, 2–4, 9–11, 17, 22, 28–30, 61, 62

Elena Alexandrovna Yablonskaya, 5, 8, 14, 15, 21, 23, 26, 27, 60

Irina Alexandrovna Zagorodnyaya, 16, 25, 42–49, 64, 65